THE LUCK HABIT

WHAT THE LUCKIEST PEOPLE THINK, KNOW AND DO... AND HOW IT CAN CHANGE YOUR LIFE

Douglas Miller

PEARSON

Harlow, England • London • New York • Boston • San Francisco • Toronto • Sydney
Auckland • Singapore • Hong Kong • Tokyo • Seoul • Taipei • New Delhi
Cape Town • São Paulo • Mexico City • Madrid • Amsterdam • Munich • Paris • Milan

PEARSON EDUCATION LIMITED

Edinburgh Gate
Harlow CM20 2JE
Tel: +44 (0)1279 623623
Fax: +44 (0)1279 431059
Website: www.pearson.com/uk

First published in Great Britain in 2012

Pearson Education is not responsible for the content of third-party internet sites.

ISBN: 978-0-273-77112-8

British Library Cataloguing-in-Publication Data
A catalogue record for this book is available from the British Library

Library of Congress Cataloging-in-Publication Data
Miller, Douglas, 1966-
   The luck habit : what the luckiest people know, say and do-- and how it can change your life / Douglas Miller. -- 1st ed.
      p. cm.
   Includes index.
   ISBN 978-0-273-77112-8 (pbk.)
   1. Fortune. I. Title.
   BF1778.M55 2012
   650.1--dc23
                                    2012015169

10 9 8 7 6 5 4 3 2 1
16 15 14 13 12

Cover image from Shutterstock.com
Design by Design Deluxe.
Typeset in 11pt Helevetica Neue Light by 30.
Printed in Great Britain by Henry Ling Ltd., at Dorset Press, Dorchester, Dorset.

Contents

About the author

DOUGLAS MILLER is a speaker, trainer, business and career coach and author. His books include *Positive Thinking, Positive Action* and *Brilliant Teams*. As a speaker and trainer he works regularly throughout the world for NGOs and NPOs and in the private sector. He travels to countries such as Haiti, Kosovo, Bosnia, 'the stans' and much of the rest of Europe. *The Luck Habit* is his eighth book.

Introduction

'I think luck is the sense to recognise an opportunity and the ability to take advantage of it. Everyone has bad breaks, but everyone also has opportunities.' SAMUEL GOLDWYN, *film producer*

Luck exists. It exists everywhere. We use the word all the time but don't usually give a lot of thought as to what it means in practice. We imply 'luck' when we use those old clichés such as 'Right place, right time' or 'Right place, wrong time' or that classic fatalistic saying 'It's not what you know, it's who you know'. Like most clichés, they do have more than a ring of truth about them. *The Luck Habit* is about accepting these as partial truisms in the sense that there are aspects of living over which you have no control. However, if you believe that 'who you know' is important then the person who has the Luck Habit will get to know 'the right people' rather than simply assuming that they don't ... and never will. And let's also acknowledge that 'what you know' is just as important as 'who you know'.

Too often, however, we confuse 'luck' with 'fate'. Fate suggests there is a guiding hand controlling not only our thoughts, actions and behaviour but also, at the extreme, all the things that happen to us in life. There are whole religions based on this very premise. Our thoughts in this book are concerned with the luck you can create and not the 'events' that would have occurred regardless of what you did or didn't do or whether you were in a particular place at a particular time.

'Fatalists' talk about luck as though some of us have it inserted into our DNA and some of us don't. We are 'born lucky' or we aren't. This blind acceptance of your fate being down to the happy meeting of a sperm and an egg (and here it is OK to say that the actual act of your own creation was down to the traditional 'old-world' definition of luck) and the consequent creation of a predetermined 'you', is frankly one of the most life-damaging mindsets you can carry with you through life.

The fatalists are never wrong. If you think that fate governs your future – whether that is because of the gifts (or lack of) you have been born with or because life is a succession of events beyond your control – you will always be proved right because you will sit back in the comfy armchair and wait for events to happen to you. They will control you because you have chosen not to control them.

TALKING TO YOURSELF

A few years ago I heard a brilliant variation of an old saying which has resonated with me ever since. It says simply:

> 'Sticks and stones may break my bones
> But words can permanently damage me'.

I heard these words on MTV and I imagine the musician who said them was thinking about words spoken by others to you. And he was right. But what we don't always consider, and what may be even more important, are the words we say to ourselves about ourselves. You and I spend huge amounts of time talking to ourselves. Those conversations that go on in our head all the time where we assess why things happened to us (or didn't happen), who controlled what happened (or didn't happen) and why we reacted in certain ways (or didn't react at all) in different situations, are very important.

This narrative gets to the heart of *The Luck Habit*. Much of *The Luck Habit* is about listening to SID (your sound inner dialogue) or, if that dialogue is currently fatalistic or merely reflective of a lack of self-belief, about changing the tone of the narrative you have with yourself. There is an example on how SID can work for you in Chapter 6 where we look at networking skills, but the idea of having a positive conversation in your own head runs through the whole book.

THE LUCK FACTORS

The first chapter of this book contains a questionnaire that introduces 20 'Luck Factors' through a series of related questions. These questions are designed to get you thinking about your own life and the way you have approached it. Specifically, these questions will draw out personal experiences to which you can apply the practical and theoretical tools in this book.

The rest of the book is built around these 20 Luck Factors. These are the things that come together to create your Luck Habit. They are spread across six chapters:

- **Chapter 2 – What Drives Luck**. This is about how to 'feel' what is right (and of course not right) for you. There's no point doing something for which you feel no affinity.

- **Chapter 3 – Learning**. Learning starts with humility – 'I don't and can't know everything' – but also great energy – '… but I want to learn as much as I can'. Your desire to learn is the very reason you picked up this book, and without that desire to learn you just won't develop and grow in the way you could.

- **Chapter 4 – Performing**. This chapter looks at how to perform beyond the level you believed you were capable, whether that is at work, at home or at play.

- **Chapter 5 – Purpose**. Whether you have a life plan, short-term goals or live in the moment, most people need a degree of purpose in their lives.

- **Chapter 6 – People**. This chapter covers specific areas – creating a network, building credibility and dealing with difficult people. It's about seeing people as a central positive focus in your life.

- **Chapter 7 – Opportunity**. There are people we think of as lucky who always seem to be presented with life's most rewarding opportunities. But this isn't luck. They are creating these opportunities themselves, both in the way they think about life and through their actions.

THE 'LUCKY' SIX

One of the things that has helped me in my life, and I am sure it is true for you as well, is to know that many of the obstacles we face are not so different from the obstacles faced by others. We all have our own versions of each other's problems. We all have our own versions of each other's opportunities too.

To help you develop the Luck Habit I have interviewed six people who have excelled in life. They are not necessarily well known, but they are great examples of how the techniques you are about to learn work in the real world. Here is a bit more about each of them:

Jonathan Bond

'You think you're doing well. Maybe you aren't.'

Jonathan is the HR director for a top UK law firm and a former *The Lawyer* magazine 'HR Director of the Year'. He has worked for global organisations in the legal and banking worlds. Jonathan likes to quote a colleague of his, for whom he has a lot of time, who says, 'If you are successful, you will have your critics'. Developing a thick skin has been important in the abrasive world of law.

Why Jonathan?

Jonathan is in the middle of a successful career. To succeed in his vocation he has had to be open to feedback on a personal level and, as he runs an internal service delivery team, he also has to be open to the wants and needs of others. His experiences have been a great help in shaping Chapter 3 'Learning' and also Chapter 4 'Performing'.

Adam Gee

'Networking is a pleasure.'

Adam is one of the most experienced commissioners in UK broadcasting of multiplatform interactive projects. He is currently multiplatform commissioning editor (factual) at Channel 4 in London. Recent projects include *The Big Fish Fight* with Hugh Fearnley-Whittingstall, *Embarrassing Bodies*, *The Great British Property Scandal* and *Jamie's Dream School*.

Adam has won over 70 international awards for his productions – including three BAFTAs, three RTS Awards, two Media Guardian Innovation Awards, a Design Council Millennium Award and the Grand Award at the New York International Film and Television Festival.

He has served on BAFTA's Television and Interactive Entertainment committees and is a voting member of the European Film Academy. He is a trustee of Culture24 and an adviser to The D Foundation and *Disorder* magazine.

Why Adam?

Adam has some great things to say about people and his relationships with them. He is a champion of creativity (of others as well as his own) and he is a formidable networker. Crucially he doesn't network for personal gain. He networks because people interest him. His views on networking are very important in Chapter 6 'People', as well as Chapter 4 'Performing', since he has a clear idea of what it is that helps him deliver.

Bernice Moran

'Listen to your heart.'

With a father who worked for Aer Lingus, it's not a surprise that Bernice developed a love of flying from a very young age. She dreamed of flying and, after overcoming a number of setbacks, she achieved that dream, becoming Europe's youngest female captain when she took the helm for Ryanair. The dream continued. Harbouring a desire to work for Virgin, eight years on she now flies Boeing 747s for Virgin Atlantic. Bernice has not been 'lucky'. What passages in the book show is that she has needed determination, hard work and clear thinking to get where she is. Bernice is also a businesswoman, running a company that provides confectionery for special occasions.

Why Bernice?

Bernice has successfully combined two crucial elements in the development of the Luck Habit – the ability to listen to her heart (the young girl's dream) and to combine this with the clear thinking needed to help her achieve a specific goal (as outlined in Chapter 5 'Purpose').

Mo Nazam

'I could have thrown my toys out of the pram.'

Mo Nazam is an internationally renowned guitarist and music teacher. He was in the vanguard of the revival of the British jazz movement in the 1980s, playing with the seminal group the Jazz Warriors and performing in many other groups and doing session work for pop artists. He has also performed in London's Royal Festival Hall and many other top venues around the world. He currently leads the Berakah Project, which brings together musicians of diverse cultural, faith and musical backgrounds. In recent years he has been a regular contributor to *Guitarist* magazine and for nearly a decade was tutor and music workshop leader for The Prince's Trust. His work with them, as well as having played for the Queen and Prince Charles as part of Keith Waithe's Macusi Players, led to an invitation to an event at Buckingham Palace in 2005 to celebrate the contribution of music to the cultural life of the UK.

Why Mo?

Mo has worked very, very hard to be good at what he does. He has had setbacks – things that could have easily diverted him away from his first love, but he stayed true to his course. His experiences of overcoming those setbacks are outlined in Chapter 3 'Learning'.

Michele Rigby

> *'If I recognised that I was demotivated I would do some-thing about it. It would be like a living death.'*

Michele is a leading champion of social enterprises – those fantastic businesses that combine a great commercial idea with the desire to help society. In 1995 she co-founded Recycle-IT! – a business that employed people who would have really struggled to get a job elsewhere.

After ten years as the MD of Recycle-IT!, Michele went on to share her knowledge through a number of directorships, including acting as a founding member of RREUSE, a network of social enterprises in the recycling industry. She served on the executive committee of its foundation from 2001 to 2006. She has also served on the DTI Small Business Council, was a director of Investors in People, and CEO of Social Enterprise East of England.

She is now chief executive of Social Firms UK, a national support and membership organisation for businesses that exists to increase employment opportunities for people who are socially disadvantaged and/or disabled.

Michele's experience informs her clear views on the needs of social enterprises and the policy directions that enable and encourage social enterprises to occupy a proper space within the national economy, and to bring new ways of effecting social change. She is a true 'social entrepreneur'.

Why Michele?

Michele has had to be sensitive to opportunities within the context of her area of work. Her experiences play an important part in shaping Chapter 7 'Opportunity'.

Greg Searle MBE

'When I challenge now, I am choosy.'

Success as a rower came quickly to Greg Searle. From being a world junior champion in 1989 and 1990, in 1992 (at the age of 20) he became an Olympic champion, alongside brother Jonny and cox Garry Herbert in the coxed pairs event. The success continued. He was world champion again in

1993, gained medals in further World Championships and won a bronze in the 1996 Olympics. And then perhaps a watershed moment came in the 2000 Olympics, where, expecting to win a medal and perhaps gold, he and his partner in the boat *Ed Coode* came fourth. Reflecting, he says: 'Things might not go the way I want. I am not bulletproof. I can get shot down. It was an important lesson.'

After rowing for a while longer, he took a different path and spent a year with *GBR Challenge* in the America's Cup yachting event. After 2002, competitive sport played less of a role in his life until 2009 when, excited by the idea of the 2012 Olympics coming to London, he came out of retirement, got himself very fit and won a place in the British rowing eight to compete in the Games. And he did this at the age of 40, which is well beyond the age where, in physically demanding sports, you could expect to succeed as a world-class performer. He and his team won successive silver medals at the 2010 and 2011 World Championships and from there it was on to 2012 …

Why Greg?

Greg won a gold medal when he was very young and eager. He still performs at an elite level but the naivety has gone and has been replaced by wisdom. His success at an elite level over a period of 20 years has given him both a high degree of self-awareness (which provides vital input into Chapter 4 'Performing') and also expertise in operating with a group of people on whom he is totally dependent (which is expanded in Chapter 6 'People').

CHAPTER 1

The Luck Factors

'Of course "luck" comes into it – it's all part of the "num-bers game". What's important to be conscious of is, if you prepare the ground properly, do the best you can, and you pay attention to the detail, you give yourself the best chance of success and being blessed with that luck.' ADAM

In the world of *The Luck Habit* we see luck not as some mystical gift from the gods of fate, but as something *you* create. By learning about the things that underpin this more achievable definition of luck, you will put yourself in the position to become the luckiest person you know.

THE 20 LUCK FACTORS

Luck is created through the use of a variety of tools, which I call the Luck Factors. These are the backbone of this book. To introduce them I have developed the questionnaire in this chapter, which will help you link each Luck Factor to your own life. This is important because you will find the book a much richer and more rewarding experience if you can relate what's said to your own personal experiences.

THE LUCK HABIT QUESTIONNAIRE

Look at the statements linked to each Luck Factor. For most statements you simply need to say yes or no, although the first two require you to produce short lists. Some statements are factual and easy to answer, some might require a bit more thought. As you go along you'll learn more about the relationship between these statements and each of the Luck Factors.

Here is some initial advice:

- Be honest about the answer – don't dally with wishful thinking.

- You'll find this a more powerful exercise if you relate your answer to a specific experience in your life. You might also find it useful to make a note of that experience next to the statement. You can use these experiences as a reference point when you read about each Luck Factor in more detail in the following chapters.

- If you are currently finding life particularly good or difficult this can create a bias in your answers that won't truly reflect your normal life. So it's important to bear this in mind and find the answer that represents your life in general too.

So, let's explore the 20 Luck Factors.

WHAT DRIVES LUCK

Luck Factor 1 – Knowing what matters to you

The first step in creating your Luck Habit is gaining an understanding of who you are and what's important to you. Developing your self-awareness enables you to focus your time and energy on the things that matter to you, both at work and play. And that focus and energy will drive you to higher and higher levels of success.

1 List the things you most enjoy about work:

_____

_____

_____

_____

_____

2 Now list the things you particularly enjoy about a hobby or pursuit you have:

_____

_____

_____

_____

_____

> ### *What's your point?*
>
> How easy was it to do these lists? Did you find the second one easier than the first? Thinking about the things you enjoy both at work and at home is a simple but effective way to focus in on those things that matter to you. You may not be able to turn a hobby into work, but if you know that you get a real energy boost from conquering a new challenge in that hobby, you may be able to find ways to replicate that in your work life.

Luck Factor 2 – Feeling eager and alive

If something has meaning for you then you will find it easier to tune yourself into it and be more excited by the possibilities it offers. You have probably noticed that when you are engaged with something then your imagination opens up, opportunities present themselves and time flies by. This engagement creates a stimulus in you. You become more sensitised to what's around you and see opportunity where others don't because, quite simply, you want to.

1 At least three days out of five I enjoy being at work.

   YES .   NO

> ### *What's your point?*
>
> The Luck Habit thrives when you have engagement with what you are doing rather than detachment. You see more because you want to see more. Adversity can bring the best out of you, drudgery won't.

2 Sometimes I have felt that there was too much going on in my life but it still felt better than the times when nothing seemed to happen.

YES   NO

What's your point?

Knowing the difference between tuned in and tuned out of the world – and preferring to be tuned in – can have its downside when everything happens at the same time. But the 'alive' feeling we get in this state is essential for a happy, fulfilled life.

---

3 Life's too short to be just passing through.

YES   NO

What's your point?

OK – not so specific, I know, but do you get the meaning behind this statement? As the years roll off the production line you might suddenly say 'What was that?' And the reply comes 'That was your life, my friend'. This is about drift. Sofa, take-away and telly is great once a week but it can easily become a habit. Don't let large chunks of your life disappear in the banality of mere existence.

Luck Factor 3 – Can do, will do

Success in life is driven by a combination of knowledge and skills – can do – and motivation – will do. One feeds the other, although everything begins with the inner flame of motivation that propels you to make the necessary commitment to action that the Luck Habit overall requires.

1 I am only working so that I can get my pension.

YES   NO

What's your point?

If that is all you want, that is probably all you will get. Spending 80–100,000 hours at work during your lifetime is an awfully long time to spend in pursuit of one thing. The psychologically retired do not tend to get much out of their work. Finding reasons to get out of bed in the morning will help you find meaning in your work, and open your eyes to the opportunities that your work has to offer – and that extends beyond the obvious motivators such as money. You can be psychologically retired at the age of 25 … and of course many terrific people are never psychologically retired from the world, regardless of their age.

---

2 I have a clear sense of what I need to learn over the next two years to keep me performing at my best.

YES   NO

> *What's your point?*
>
> The luckiest never see it as humiliation to carry on learning, regardless of age. They recognise that their knowledge and skills always need updating.

LEARNING

Luck Factor 4 – Failure is good

Failure is a very necessary part of life. Not only does every setback have lessons to teach you about why you might fail, it also shows you how your response can lead to greater success, if you are willing to learn the lessons it has to teach.

1 I think that the past is for learning and the future is for living.

YES   NO

> *What's your point?*
>
> We all fail, all the time, but (as Chapter 3 says) without failure success is not an option. People with the Luck Habit seem to understand that failure is a necessary route to success and not definitive proof that you are not now, and never will be, good enough. It is too easy to get paralysed by the failures of the past rather than the possibilities of the future. Can you think of an example of something in your own life for which, at first, you seemed to lack basic ability but through purposeful, persistent practice you got yourself to a good level?

Perhaps a hobby that you took up when you were young? Remember, too, that the better you get at something, the more opportunities seem to open up for you to get even better.

2 I have failed at something more than once (for example, the driving test) before I succeeded.

YES   NO

What's your point?

If you want to do something enough you can take any amount of failure in order to succeed, and you've probably proved that at least once in your life. Where else can you apply this liberating mindset?

Luck Factor 5 – Knowing your capability

So, beyond your current set of skills, do you know what else you could be capable of? It's so easy to get stuck with a nice comfortable set of competencies and lose the curiosity to seek out new skills. But that way lies stagnation and boredom, and increasingly your abilities will become irrelevant as the world spins on without your involvement. To be lucky you have to be curious and experiment with new things. Otherwise you will never know what else you could be capable of.

1 I can think of a time when I have tried something new and been surprised that I could do it better than I thought.

    YES   NO

What's your point?

This is not because of that fatalist excuse for success – beginner's luck. You succeeded because you are capable of succeeding, not because of some mystical notion that the God of Beginner's Luck happened to be shining his light on you at that moment.

---

2 If I think about the things I can do now, I think my past self (five to ten years ago) would be pleasantly surprised.

    YES   NO

What's your point?

Of course, improvements and successes are important for confidence building, but they also provide a provable record that we can all perform better than we may have previously imagined.

Luck Factor 6 – Being open to feedback

Whether praise or criticism, feedback is a *gift* and it is up to you what you do with it. Rather than instantly accepting or rejecting what has been said, or committing yourself to ill-thought-out actions, do take time to consider the feedback and choose the best response and course of action.

1 I have resented feedback that has been given to me, but with hindsight I can see that the feedback-giver had a point.

YES   NO

What's your point?

Being told things about yourself that surprise you or which you think but didn't think anyone else knew can produce an emotional, instant 'I reject this' reaction. The secret is never to take feedback personally (even if it was given that way).

---

2 I sometimes get embarrassed when people praise me.

YES   NO

What's your point?

This is surprisingly common. Have you ever found yourself saying 'It was nothing really' when clearly something was done well? Don't dismiss the praise. Enjoy it and remember how you accomplished the task, as success is as valuable a teacher as failure.

Luck Factor 7 – Modelling your learning

Some people see the success of others as a reason to knock their own confidence. But there is no reason why you shouldn't be thinking 'They are good, so there is no reason why I can't be good too'.

1 I like to see others succeed and I can think of an occasion when I have used the success of others to motivate me.

YES   NO

What's your point?

Are you jealous of the success of others – 'Why him and not me'? Jealousy can be a paralysing emotional response. The excellence of others should be motivating and not diminishing for you. You can use it as a spur to your own endeavours – a demonstration of the art of the possible: 'It's great to see her doing well. What is she doing or thinking that I am not?'

The next two statements refer to a particular aspect of learning – what I call 'humble intelligence':

2 I can recall a specific example, from the last six months, when I have said to someone (when I don't know or understand something): 'I don't know, can you tell me?'

YES   NO

What's your point?

It is easier to say 'I don't know' to ourselves than it is to say it to others, but some people can't even take this step. If you are not prepared to admit that you don't know something, you will lack the curiosity to go and find the answer and gain more knowledge.

---

3 If I find I don't know something I go straight to the internet, a book etc. to find the answer. Or I ask someone.

YES   NO

What's your point?

Do you rationalise this as 'I don't know the answer, therefore I am stupid' (i.e. reinforcement of low self-worth) *or* 'I don't know the answer, I don't know everything (and wouldn't that be boring), but I want to find out'? In other words intelligence is about a willingness to understand rather than a blinkered view about your inferior or superior intellect.

The most intelligent people can also be the most limited in their thinking. Some intelligent people rationalise much of the world as 'I am intelligent, therefore I am right'. It's a major barrier. It can start in the late teenage years where intelligent children who have formed their world-view by the age of 18 find it very difficult to challenge that view later in life.

Luck Factor 8 – Turning fear into fulfilment

This Luck Factor is about being able to turn 'anticipation anxiety' – unease or fear about a forthcoming event – into a successful experience. How you talk yourself into or out of a potential positive experience is what matters here.

1 I have been very nervous about a forthcoming experience – for example, having to 'mix and mingle' in an environment where I don't know anybody, or making a presentation.

    YES   NO

2 I can think of a time where, although I was anxious about a forthcoming experience, it wasn't as bad as I thought it was going to be. (Again – can you think of a specific experience?)

    YES   NO

What's your point?

We all have our own individual fears. Often these fears become self-fulfilling prophecies. You feel anxious about something, the conversation you have in your head makes you even more anxious about it and those anxieties are played out in your behaviour. Sometimes it is also easy to generalise – for example, has every 'mix and mingle' event or every presentation been a terrible experience? I'm ready to bet not. So what made the good ones work?

PERFORMING

Luck Factor 9 – Hard work

Lazy people don't have the Luck Habit. But this isn't just about getting your nose to the grindstone and keeping it there. The best performers know where they need to focus their efforts for the biggest gains and they create a sense of purpose behind the hard work and continually practise to improve their performance.

1 I am aware of the things I am talented at and the things I am not.

YES   NO

> **What's your point?**
>
> If you rely on talent to succeed you are letting fate (the gifts you were born with) control you. Successful people know that while talent helps, what makes the difference is hard work.

2 If I want to be good at anything I need to practise.

YES   NO

> **What's your point?**
>
> So, building on the last point, what makes the difference is hard work combined with practice. Talent is fixed. Hard work with practice has no fixed outcome.

Luck Factor 10 – What's the point?

Put simply, this Luck Factor is about understanding the value you add and what you are here to do.

1 When I think about a group of people I am a part of (for example, a work or sports team) I am clear about what I bring to the group.

YES   NO

What's your point?

We are a part of a group because we bring specific skills to the group, for example, the actual position you play in a sports team or your technical knowledge at work. You also bring skills that are less tangible – are you a good ideas person, relationship-centred, a leader?

---

2 Without too much thinking, I know what others want from me when I am working with them (this could refer to your team at work, your customers, your boss, or the people you know via social activities, sports or hobbies).

YES   NO

What's your point?

The most successful people are clear about what it is they do or offer – the 'point' of their performance. At work this shouldn't be confined to the rigidity of the job description. What is it that you should be doing that really gets to the heart of delivering top performance?

Luck Factor 11 – Thinking without thinking

This Luck Factor is about your route to more open-minded thinking and the conditions in which you have your best thoughts. It's about slowing down your mind to let your best thoughts catch up with you.

1 I know when I have my best ideas. And I can make a quick list of those occasions now.

YES   NO

_____

_____

_____

_____

_____

What's your point?

We often have our best ideas when we aren't consciously thinking about a problem. In fact many of us have our best ideas when we are in the shower or out walking or swimming. In other words when our brain is relaxed.

---

2 I write down my ideas – even at 3.00 a.m.

YES   NO

What's your point?

Are your ideas easily forgotten flights of fantasy, or do you take your ideas seriously? Seriously enough that you want to capture them? A friend of mine once installed a whiteboard in his shower so that he could record his thoughts as his brain relaxed into problem-solving mode. That's serious.

3 When I do a Google search, I have a look at page 20 or page 30 of the search answers as a matter of habit.

YES   NO

What's your point?

The point here is that many of us look for the obvious things in the obvious places – the places where everyone else is looking. On Google the straightforward answers come on the first two pages – many of the really interesting ones are on subsequent pages. So the question for you is: 'Do you look for interesting things in strange or different places?'

Luck Factor 12 – Keeping fresh

Relentlessly focusing on one thing will only make you go cross-eyed. You will quickly find you've become jaded and lacklustre. Lucky people are curious – they hunt out new experiences and different ways of doing things and keep their thinking fresh.

1 I have had a 'holiday at home' in the last 12 months (if you don't understand the statement, say no).

YES   NO

What's your point?

Familiarity with your immediate surroundings leads you to taking those surroundings for granted. Which leads to missing out on what those surroundings have to offer. This applies equally to work and, yes, holidays too. To see your surroundings in new ways, become a tourist in your own neighbourhood.

---

2 I can clearly remember the *last time* I did something for the *first time*. (If an answer doesn't come to you in 10 seconds, put no.)

YES   NO

What's your point?

A willingness to try new things lies at the heart of opportunity seeking and therefore of the Luck Habit. But this is a bit more than just willingness. It is also about an active search for new, first-time experiences. It is the next step on from the point made in the previous questions.

---

3 I try to take different routes to work – even occasionally.

YES   NO

What's your point?

Taking a different route to work is one small way in which you can break your routine. There are many others – not only could you take a different route but you could also take a different mode of transport. Routine-breaking helps you to keep yourself and your thinking fresh.

---

4 Trying new things gives me 'a feeling of being alive' – it's what life is all about.

    YES   NO

What's your point?

It's perfectly OK not to want to do this. Lots of people like stability and routine. But the Luck Habit needs proactivity and at least a small spirit of adventure.

PURPOSE

Luck Factor 13 – Having life-defining goals

All the Luck Factors are optional of course, but this one is probably more optional than the others. Some people thrive on life plans and big goals – one of our interviewees, Bernice Moran, has pursued a big life goal for nearly 30 years. Others find this doesn't suit them and prefer shorter-term thinking or even, as we will see in Luck Factor 15, to 'live in the moment'. There is no right answer. If big goals aren't motivating for you, don't bother with them. If the big life project is right for you, then great. So here self-awareness is required.

1 I had a life plan before the age of 20.

YES   NO

2 I have had a life plan at certain stages of my life which, although I didn't see it/them through, provided direction for me for a period of time.

YES   NO

What's your point?

Some people do have a life plan developed before the age of 20 which they see through. Many of us might have had dreams or fantasies before that age which remained as dreams – we didn't act. Action usually requires clear thinking – the development of a long-term strategy to achieve the big life goals. But, just like the short-term goals of Luck Factor 14, the big life plan can provide life purpose for some people.

Luck Factor 14 – Having a horizon

The big life goals can be hard to motivate if the pinnacle of achievement is a long way in the future. Short-term goals provide an instantly accessible means of creating purpose and monitoring progress. Hence the name of this Luck Factor.

1 I set myself short-term goals to help me improve. (Can you think of a specific example of when you have done this in the last 12 months?)

YES   NO

What's your point?

Setting short-term goals makes the big stuff manageable. These milestones are also a good way to monitor progress.

---

2 I know what it takes to mentally stimulate me and I make sure I have projects ahead of me that provide that stimulation.

YES   NO

What's your point?

Short-term goals are great, but they must have meaning for you.

Luck Factor 15 – Living in the moment

This Luck Factor is not meant to be a total philosophy for life, but it should be part of life. It suggests that there are times when we need to run with the heart rather than the analysing head.

1 I regularly take a step back and think about the things I have enjoyed in the day, as well as the problems.

YES   NO

What's your point?

It's easy to forget the simple pleasures – or even not to notice them – when you're wrapped up in all in the other stuff.

2 I sometimes act impulsively.

YES   NO

What's your point?

Moments of spontaneity are a crucial part of life. Even with the clearly thought-through approaches suggested in this book, too much rigidity will mean missing out on opportunity and fun.

PEOPLE

Luck Factor 16 – Behaviour breeds behaviour

There are always people we don't get on with at first but learn to rub along with in the end. There are also people that we will never get on with. But there are things we can do to keep the second group of people as small as possible. Your good behaviour gives you the best chance of that behaviour being reciprocated.

1 I can think of a few people I have come across who I couldn't stand. No way could I work with them.

    YES   NO

2 I can think of a few people in my life who, although I didn't particularly like, I have learned to accommodate.

    YES   NO

What's your point?

Some people seem to have rather more people they 'can't stand' than others in their lives. Perhaps this type of person needs to address their personal style rather than point the finger at others.

Luck Factor 17 – Networking

This Luck Factor is about building networks with the best of intentions. It is about seeing networking as a pleasure and not something you only do for what you can get out of it. Statement 3 is a good indicator of this healthy practice.

1 I work hard at cultivating a network of contacts – and not just LinkedIn contacts.

    YES   NO

What's your point?

LinkedIn is fine, but unless you are a really active user it can be a very passive networking tool. Having a list of close contacts is good. But a good networker will also think of contacts where the relationship can be further developed and with people they barely know at all. That often means face-to-face contact.

2 I don't drop friends and contacts – if I'm in the neighbourhood I get in touch, even if I haven't seen them for ages.

    YES   NO

What's your point?

I picked this tip up from Adam – one of the interviewees in this book and a supreme networker. Lapsing time should not be a reason to lose people you get on with.

3 I enjoy bringing people together who I think might be able to help each other.

    YES   NO

What's your point?

This is important because actions like this show that you network to help others and not just for quick results that only benefit yourself. In fact this kind of networking does reap rewards for you in the longer term because people remember what you did.

Luck Factor 18 – Influencing

Reputation and trust are two of the main sources of influence available to you. Many of the most effective people have to get results through people and for that they need to exercise influence. This Luck Factor shows how to grow that influence.

1 I am clear about the kind of reputation I have and why I have that reputation.

YES   NO

What's your point?

Some people are very accurate about their reputation, others are very wrong (and of course the ones who are so wrong think they are so right). But it is clear that reputation – and by that I mean good rather than notorious – is a major means to have influence, to persuade and to negotiate.

---

2 I use the words 'Trust me' in conversation.

YES   NO

What's your point?

Trust is a major source of power and influence for you. It takes time to build this. If anyone uses the words 'Trust me' as a means of influencing me I am automatically suspicious of the reasons why I am being told to do this. Those who have real influence do not have to remind anyone of the source of that influence.

Luck Factor 19 – Sharing success

This is all about the atmosphere between you and others and the three very simple things you can do to create a better one – give praise, say thank you and celebrate success.

1 I have congratulated someone on their success in the last three months.

    YES   NO

What's your point?

People agonise over problems and failure – if you work in an office you probably find that meetings seem to be about nothing else – and don't champion success enough. Commenting on the success of others is a very healthy way of building a relationship – people like it that you have noticed.

---

2 I have made a point of thanking someone for something they have done for me in the last seven days.

    YES   NO

What's your point?

Thanks and praise are a great way of making people feel good about themselves (as well as a primary motivator) and we remember the people who've noticed us. But the longer we are around the same people the more we tend to take each other for granted. Take time to remember.

OPPORTUNITY

Luck Factor 20 – Spotting opportunities

People with the Luck Habit don't wait for opportunities to 'pass by'. They are active in engineering them for themselves, and are 'primed' to take advantage of opportunities when they do appear.

1 I see multiple options in any given situation rather than the perfect 'single right answer'.

YES   NO

What's your point?

As human beings we have a tendency to look for the perfect cognitive response – the single right answer which is often also the most obvious one. There are often many possibilities and therefore many right answers.

---

2 In the last 12 months I can think of a time when someone has laughed at an idea I have had.

YES   NO

What's your point?

Most of us don't enjoy embarrassment. On the other hand, as the truism tells us, only fools never appear foolish. Other people's laughter can be a reflection of their own lack of enjoyment of creative insight rather than your foolishness, or it could be that they just love your playfulness. Enjoy the play involved in opening up your imagination. Opportunity spotters have a thick skin. Today's laughable idea is tomorrow's success story.

3 I know what the highest point is in my local town or village – and I have been there!

YES   NO

What's your point?

Can you see your immediate surroundings – both physical and psychological – in different ways? This is really a metaphorical question about curiosity. Opportunity spotters ask questions like – 'How can I do this better, cheaper, quickly, differently?'.

4 If nothing seems to happen, I make something happen.

YES   NO

What's your point?

Entrepreneur and boxer George Foreman once said that he thought that 'nothing' would be the worst thing he could imagine happening to him. Opportunity spotters are rarely satisfied with the cosy status quo.

5 I look 'up' when walking down the street and not just at things at eye-level.

> YES   NO

What's your point?

This is a metaphor for the importance of 'widening your gaze'. Actually it is not a just a metaphor – you do see great things when you look up as well as at eye-level. Possibilities – which are what opportunities are – reveal themselves in abundance if you are prepared to look in different places to find them.

---

6 I can think of one time in my life when I made a life-changing decision in a few minutes because it felt right.

> YES   NO

What's your point?

There is danger in this – our feelings can emotionally contaminate good decision making. But as a principle it is true that there are occasions when opportunities are so fleeting that we don't have time for considered contemplation. Sometimes it pays to listen to your heart as well your head. When I work with groups to help them make better decisions it is interesting how many people say that these rapid decisions are sometimes among the best decisions they have ever made. And anyway it is better to act on a decision you are emotionally committed to than the rationally thought-through decision for which you feel no emotional propulsion.

THE 20 LUCK FACTORS

So here now is a list of all 20 Luck Factors:

- **What drives luck**

  Luck Factor 1 – Knowing what matters to you

  Luck Factor 2 – Feeling eager and alive

  Luck Factor 3 – Can do, will do

- **Learning**

  Luck Factor 4 – Failure is good

  Luck Factor 5 – Knowing your capability

  Luck Factor 6 – Being open to feedback

  Luck Factor 7 – Modelling your learning

  Luck Factor 8 – Turning fear into fulfilment

- **Performing**

  Luck Factor 9 – Hard work

  Luck Factor 10 – What's the point?

  Luck Factor 11 – Thinking without thinking

  Luck Factor 12 – Keeping fresh

- **Purpose**

  Luck Factor 13 – Having life-defining goals

  Luck Factor 14 – Having a horizon

  Luck Factor 15 – Living in the moment

- **People**

  Luck Factor 16 – Behaviour breeds behaviour

  Luck Factor 17 – Networking

CHAPTER 2

What Drives Luck

'What am I going to do now, learn to play golf? ... I want to feel like I used to feel. All eager and alive.' DEL-BOY, *Only Fools and Horses,* BBC TV

Luck Factors in this chapter:

Luck Factor 1 – Knowing what matters to you

Luck Factor 2 – Feeling eager and alive

Luck Factor 3 – Can do, will do

Television comedy is often funny because the lines reveal a lot about us to ourselves. We've said or done some of the things we observe and can laugh at the ridiculousness of it all. Sometimes, however, it is the serious lines between the comedy that say even more.

In the classic British sit-com *Only Fools and Horses* the leading character Del-boy, the hard-working street-trader selling 'dodgy' goods out of a suitcase, has, with his brother, suddenly become a multi-millionaire through the auctioning of a rare eighteenth-century pocket watch which had been left lying around in their garage because they thought it was a Victorian egg-timer. He no longer needs to work. With all this sudden wealth, Del-boy is struggling to define what it is that is lacking in his life. In a poignant moment, he says to his brother: 'What am I going to do now, learn to play golf? … I want to feel like I used to feel. All eager and alive.'

You cannot succeed at work or life if you do not have that eager and alive feeling. It comes from occupying yourself, and deciding what is right for you and the kind of person you are, combined with the motivation, knowledge and skills that you have that enable you to do something well. Or, put more succinctly, the two factors that will determine your success are:

- **Affinity**: Does it feel right?
- **Performance**: Can you do it … and do it well?

And the first drives the second. In this chapter we'll look at the first three Luck Factors, which are all about finding this affinity for what you do.

LUCK FACTOR 1 – KNOWING WHAT MATTERS TO YOU

'I oscillate – sometimes I feel I know nothing and at other times I feel like I am one of the best at doing this. Sometimes I look objectively and say "It's just telly, it's not life or death" and other times I feel "Wow, that's had a real impact on the world and made things better". For example, with The Big Fish Fight there's been a real *impact on European policy and on supermarket sourc-ing which will make the chances of there being edible fish in the sea when my children are grown up significantly higher. That means a lot to me. It's fuel to my fire.'* ADAM

The first question in the Luck Habit questionnaire came in two parts:

1 List the things you most enjoy about work.

2 Now list the things you particularly enjoy about a hobby or pursuit you have.

It is easy to fall into the work = bad, play = good trap here. Your answers to the work question may be along the lines of: regular challenges, earning money, meeting new people, the responsibility, so I can test myself, developing knowledge and skills. There are many other possibilities.

Your answers to the hobbies/interests question may not be so different but, if you don't particularly enjoy your job, there may be more of them. You can try asking the same questions and insert the word 'don't' as in 'don't particularly enjoy'. If there is a disconnect with your work then the work list might be substantial. In fact what you may find yourself doing is deliberately producing a long list so as to reinforce the point that your primary occupation is not engaging you.

When I asked Greg and Adam the same question their answers suggested a strong degree of self-awareness. For Greg his primal competitive instinct needs to be nourished. For Adam, putting himself in a position where he can make an impact on the world is: 'fuel to my fire'.

Finding the thing that drives you is at the very heart of what life and living are all about. Some would go further and say that it gets to the heart of what being a human being is all about.

It comes back to the old question you may have come across: 'Who are you being when you are doing what you are doing?' If you are being true to yourself, you can happily say 'I am being me', which is great. But if you are not being true to yourself then you will feel disconnected with and unfulfilled by what you do. And if you're looking at this in a work context, that amounts to 80–120,000 hours of your life.

Identifying strengths and values

'So, what has helped me get to this stage of my career? Well, whatever role you undertake you have to be motivated to take that role. Don't just do it because it sounds good. At an earlier stage in my career I found myself asking, "Is this right for me?" A sign that perhaps it wasn't or that I needed to move on.' JONATHAN

Psychologists talk of the masks we wear that present a compromise between the 'real me' – the strengths, values, vulnerabilities and even weaknesses that everyone has – and the face you have to present to the outside world in order to get along, develop relationships (even with a life partner) and succeed at work. In order to feel affinity with what you do you need to reconcile these two things in the context of the groups you are involved with. Let's take a closer look at these three elements:

1 **The real me**. It's important to develop a very clear sense of what is important to you. This will be driven by your core values, which are the things you really care about

and which make you 'ert' rather than 'inert'. Your values provide the test for the rightness of the direction you are choosing to take. In other words they will warn you if you are heading off in a direction that is not right for you. I recommend a visit to Dr Martin Seligman's website: **www.authentichappiness.com**. On it you will find the VIA Survey of Character Strengths which will help you to identify the areas that are important to you. He refers to what he calls your Signature Strengths – these are typically the five top strengths you have out of a well-researched list of 24. These might include, for example, 'fairness', 'leadership', 'integrity' and 'perseverance'. Happiness in what you do in life – work, hobbies, home – tends to come from regularly accessing these five Signature Strengths.

2 **The group**. Many organisations, groups and teams have a clear stated set of values that are designed to unite everyone. Whether this group is at work, a sporting team, an amateur dramatics group or choir, you will have to reconcile your values with those of the group. Sometimes these group values are written down somewhere, perhaps in a mission statement at work or in the induction pack you get from a new society you've joined. The group's real values become apparent when you watch the action and vocabulary of the people within that group.

3 **My role (the mask)**. We all play myriad different roles. At work we may be required to be conscientious, innovative, highly productive, etc. At home we have different roles to play with our friends and family. Sometimes these roles are written down for us in job descriptions. But often there is a more subtle expectation of us that we have to fulfil.

What you are searching for is congruence between these three elements, because the chemistry created between them is crucial in establishing the affinity you have with the task at hand. A high level of congruence leads to a closer affinity and allows you to access the eager and alive feeling we all love (see Luck Factor 2).

With activities beyond work we often do this instinctively. You decide to join a swimming club, for example, because fitness and health are important to you, but you also quite enjoy the solitude that swimming provides. The club offers this and in addition brings you into contact with people who have a similar set of needs, priorities and values.

So, let's get down to the nitty gritty of how this can work for you. Below are two alternative exercises. The first requires you to play intellectually a little with the concept of your values, and needs some depth in your thinking. The second uses three circles to illustrate affinity.

GETTING DRESSED

Below you see a mannequin. The mannequin, in its naked form, is 'the real me'. The first thing you need to do is clothe your mannequin.

These clothes represent 'the group'. Think of the group you want to illustrate – as an example let's look at work. What is your mannequin wearing and how does it fit? For example, a traditional business suit would indicate a group that adheres to more sober, controlled values, whereas more colourful, casual, imaginative clothes would represent a group that values creativity and a more relaxed environment. What about the belt? A tight belt might suggest that you are being required to work in a restricted, controlled, supervised manner. Fine, if that's what you like (and a lot of people do), but not so good if you don't. Trainers – perhaps fast-moving? Overall do the clothes fit the mannequin well, i.e. are they right for you?

Now we come to the third element – the hat (if you wish to keep the term 'the mask', then do so). You've probably heard this used as a metaphor. People talk of the 'hats' they have to wear at work: 'Wearing my managerial hat ...' Is it ill-fitting? Does it clash with the clothes? Is it big – is the role you play an important one? Does the hat match the clothes and fit on the head of the mannequin? If it does, then you have a nice overall look. And, more importantly, a good match between the real you, the group and the role you are playing.

You don't feel that your current role is quite right for you.

Perhaps your organisation keeps its employees under a tight rein.

THREE CIRCLES

This is an alternative to the mannequin exercise and you may prefer this if detailed drawing isn't your thing. In this method the three elements (the real me, the group, and my role) are reprised but this time are represented by three circles:

A The real me

B The group/department/organisation

C My role

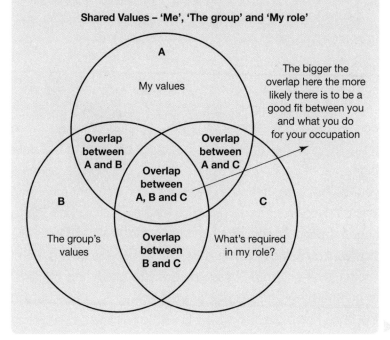

Shared Values – 'Me', 'The group' and 'My role'

The degree to which the circles overlap gives you the extent to which there is a match between the three elements. It is possible to have the three circles not meeting at all, which suggests a serious disconnect between you, the organisation/group and the role you are required to perform. A perfect fit would mean the three circles sit on top of each other.

You might find it easiest to start by identifying where the commonality exists between A and C, B and C and then A and B. This should help you then to identify the commonality between A, B and C. It's good to start on a positive note. After this you can look at the things that are unique to each element.

Compromise

The level of compatibility you have with your occupation will depend on the match or indeed mismatch between these three things. That occupation need not be confined to your formal job. It could refer to particular hobbies you have where you are either contemplating a deeper commitment time-wise and emotionally or considering starting something new. (With activities beyond work, we often have this affinity instinctively.) However, seeking happiness in your occupation will depend on the level of compromise you *have* to make and the level of compromise you are *prepared* to make. So, this is where the Luck Habit begins. It begins with affinity and connection with what you are doing. This affinity sensitises you to the possibilities that your occupation has to offer which will simply not exist if there is a disconnection. It comes back to the old question raised earlier in this chapter: 'Who are you being when you are doing what you are doing?' If you are not being true to yourself to a reasonable extent then you are unlikely to be engaged by what you do. You won't be very happy either.

Knowing what matters to you – summary

- Be clear about what's important to you, for example, your values.

- Understand the values espoused by your group – your employer, club etc.

- Know what's expected of you in your role – what 'hat' do you have to wear?

- Evaluate the match between the three elements – the real you, the group, your role.

- Be prepared to make some compromises – seeking perfection will lead to its own form of unhappiness.

- Resolve to do something about any mismatch, remembering that you can access the things that mean something for you in another part of your life.

LUCK FACTOR 2 – FEELING EAGER AND ALIVE

'It is not necessarily about rowing. What I enjoy is competition. I definitely enjoy training – the good feeling I get from it makes it worthwhile. And even when the training is painful it is a small price to pay for being able to do this.' GREG

'It's a magnificent feeling when I sit in that seat. I'm flying 400 tons in weight, with 500 people on the plane. And when I go from auto-pilot to manual hand-control … well, it's hard to express what a great feeling that is. It's a cliché but I have to say it's a bit like a lottery-win feeling.' BERNICE

When you are working on something that doesn't engage you, you know right away. You may be the person who 'hangs in there' because certain aspects of your job (for example, the friendships you develop at work) sustain you just enough to help you through the chunks of the work you don't like. But really is that enough? Equally you'll know when you are feeling 'eager and alive' about something – that sense of everything connecting together, of energy pulsing through you and the excitement you feel just before you begin, followed by a sense of flow while you are in the midst of it.

Here are four subjective 'tests' to help you assess the likelihood of this in your own working life:

1 Do you have three or more days per week when you consciously look forward ('eager') to your daytime occupation when you get up in the morning?
2 Can you imagine a life not doing what you are doing?
3 Do you find yourself engaging *creatively* with what you are doing, i.e. generating new ideas?
4 Do you get a period of more than an hour during a single working day when you look at the clock and it is at least an hour later than you thought it was?

Let's look at each of these points in turn.

I want to be here

'If I recognised that I was demotivated I would do something about it. It would be like a living death. What is the point of not wanting to go to work? You've got to do something about it.' MICHELE

There are two categories of people who don't have an eager and alive feeling about what they do. The first group consists of those who have an entirely negative attitude to work per se. The second group is made up of people who are just doing the wrong thing for them or where, although there are things about the job they enjoy, there are rather more things they don't.

Ask people who have a hobby that they love and I am sure they will say that they have the odd day when they don't feel like getting in the pool, playing with model trains or knitting. A break, even from what you love doing, can be invigorating. It's also perfectly normal to have the odd day when you just don't feel like going to work. But when these bad days start occurring regularly, you know you have a problem. Some people tell me they have been in the same job for 20 years and they hate it. What a dreadful waste of time. I entreat them (and you, if you are in this situation) to change it, or requalify. This is a whole topic in itself and there are many good books and career coaches available to help you. Hopefully you aren't in this situation, but like most people there will be things you like about your job and things you don't like. Here are some ideas on how to feel more eager and alive.

Brains for breakfast

This is a metaphor for getting the things you don't like out of the way first thing. Then you can focus your talents on the things that engage you. Nine times out of ten these will also be the things that create success for your team and your business and that will get you noticed as a valuable member of the team, which in turn marks you out as the one likely to go on to bigger career success …

How to be

Here's the science bit. Neuroscience research has shown that when two people 'connect', electrical activity in the brain occurs in similar places in both people and neurohormones such as dopamine are released, which induce happier feelings. Some have referred to this process as our 'neural Wi-Fi' kicking in. This is why the old adage that 'Behaviour breeds behaviour' is so true.

So try this one tomorrow – it's amazing how it works. When you wake up, decide on a word that you will 'be' for the day. It could be 'interested', 'friendly', 'positive', 'helpful' or any other active word. Now be that word for the whole day and notice what happens. You'll find that the behaviour you demonstrate being that word will start to be reflected back to you by other people, even if you don't particularly feel that way to begin with. And when it gets reflected back to you, you will feel great, as will the people you interact with. Now that's a nice virtuous circle.

Suddenly – it's gone

In 2008/9 the Woolworths chain of stores in the UK closed forever – over 500 of them. Thousands of jobs were lost and an iconic name disappeared from the high street. But Claire Robertson, the manager of the Dorchester branch, refused to take it lying down and a month after the closure she reopened the store under a new name 'Wellworths' (later renamed as 'Wellchester'). The opening was covered on the national TV news bulletins and a prime-time BBC documentary gave an insider view into the weeks leading up to the grand opening.

And in the middle of this story of success against the odds there was a wonderfully touching moment when a staff member returned to her till in tears of joy because she had got her old job back, which meant so much to her. The old cliché that says 'You don't know what you've lost till it's gone' was never truer. I wonder if she had questioned the emotional importance of that job to her before the closure of the original store.

As business theorist Ichak Adizes has said:

> 'The best things in life are known by their absence. You do not know the worth of your health until you get sick, the value of love till you are lonely, or the benefits of democracy till you experience dictatorship.'

Experimentation

Creativity, playfulness and experimentation are the pleasurable side effects of true engagement with what you choose to occupy your time. When the great Olympic swimmer Ian 'Thorpedo' Thorpe was 12 he found that his times had plateaued. He wondered what might happen if he stopped kicking his legs and instead 'stretched' his stroke out further. His times were just as good as before, although swimmers are always told that the kick is crucial (which it is). With this new stretched stroke, he started to kick again and suddenly his times improved significantly. What Ian was doing was playing/experimenting as he swam. That 'play' and desire to experiment comes from curiosity. And we are only curious about the things that we are truly engaged with – those for which we feel an affinity.

In your own world, you might be asking questions like 'How do I do this better, quicker, cheaper, more easily?' This is about being open and curious about opportunity, which is, in itself, a form of creativity. If you are not doing this with the things you spend your time doing then it's a sign that you haven't got that 'eager and alive' feeling about them.

Where did the time go?

So, did you recognise that feeling? You're lost in something, you're not even thinking about whether you have enjoyed it or not (because you don't feel the need to ask the question) and you look up at the clock and it's much later than you thought. It's what's known as the state of 'flow'. You experience it with hobbies. If you are engrossed in a book or magazine, you will recognise how hours fly by (ever missed your station?). This state of flow is how people who are really tuned into what they are doing recognise the value to them of what they do. While work and play is a lot more than just collecting these flow experiences, the regularity of them is a good way of assessing how 'eager and alive' you are about what you do.

Feeling eager and alive – summary

- Self-awareness will help you really assess when you are truly connected with what you are doing and when you are just drifting.

- Do something about it when you don't enjoy what you do, or you will feel 'drift'.

- 'Am I being me?' Ask yourself who you are being when you are doing what you are doing. Are you having to be someone else?

- If you sometimes struggle to see the value of what you do, try to really think what it might be like if it was suddenly taken away.

- Curiosity is a classic sign of genuine connection and interest in many parts of your life.

- Treasure the times when you get 'lost' in what you are doing.

LUCK FACTOR 3 – CAN DO, WILL DO

Doing what is right for you and the kind of person you are (Luck Factor 1) allied to the highly sensitised state you feel from Luck Factor 2 means an increased likelihood that the third Luck Factor drops into place. Your success is likely to be dependent on the marriage of two things:

- Your knowledge and skills – 'can do'.

- Your motivation to apply that knowledge – 'will do'.

These two sub-factors can be expressed in the following model:

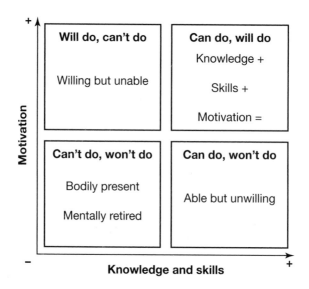

Can't do, won't do

You have probably met a few of these types – people who carry this 'bodily present, mentally retired' approach with them throughout life. Others display these characteristics at work but have a life beyond work, where they are 'can do, will do'. You yourself may well feel that you have parts of your life where you fit into the 'can't do, won't do' box but others where you are the opposite. And you are probably clear about the reasons why.

Will do, can't do

If you find yourself in this position you should find that the 'will do' will provide the emotional propulsion to help you learn quickly. The next chapter deals with learning ('can do') in detail. However, to help you assess your own needs there is a simple sequence you can follow:

- **Where should I be?** This could be based on any number of criteria.

- **What is the knowledge gap?** This is the gap between where you are now and where you need to be.

- **What is the evidence of a gap?** Use specific examples from your own performance and behaviour. Use feedback from others (see Luck Factor 6), your own practical experiences and gut feeling.

- **Why might there be a gap?** The lack of motivation may be one factor (see 'can do, won't do' below). But most importantly you must realise that you cannot know everything. Those with the Luck Habit know this and respond positively to the need to address lack of knowledge and skills. Unfortunately, those who lack confidence see any shortcoming as confirmation of an innate and permanent lack of ability. This is a damaging and wholly unnecessary mindset and it is addressed in the next chapter.

- **What are the solutions?** Knowing what you need, assuming you have the motivation to address the knowledge and skills gap, is the first step in identifying the answers to your need. Those answers will be unique to the need you have.

Can do, won't do

This can be summarised as a lack of motivation. Here are some possible reasons why this might be the case for you:

- Perhaps you feel no real affinity for what you are doing. Is it time for a change?
- Perhaps you are disengaged because there are bigger, more important issues in life for you.
- If this relates to your work only, you may just be seeing your work as a means to an end.
- Perhaps you suffer from poor relationships – addressed in Chapter 6 'People'.
- The pressure placed on you may be excessive. We can all only take so much. Aside from talking with those who place these demands on you, it is important that you have a safety valve that relieves the pressure and creates balance. See Luck Factor 9 for further ideas on this.

Can do, will do

'Can do' combined with 'will do' is a very powerful combination and is one of the defining traits of people who have the Luck Habit. 'Will do' is not a tap that can be switched on and off, though there do seem to be some people who can throw themselves into anything they try. You may have observed this behaviour yourself and noted that the energy doesn't always last. I believe strongly that the affinity covered in Luck Factor 1 and the accessing of the 'eager and alive' feeling in Luck Factor 2 goes a long way to bring out the 'will do' in you and me.

So, which is best?

'With experience, I am also able to see the benefits of the "blind optimism" I had in me at 20 when I won my first gold medal. There were always ways around problems and that's a healthy mentality. I was an Olympic gold medallist with fallibilities but I didn't see them in myself of course. And winning gave me a high level of self-esteem.' GREG

If pushed, I might say that 'will do' is best. You can go a long way with drive and determination even if your knowledge is sometimes lacking. Greg, in his quote above, identifies the power of the blind optimism that helped him win Olympic gold medals when barely into his twenties. This has been a primary force for many of us -- and probably you too. But, at some point, you will be tested. You can't ignore the 'can do' in the hope of riding the 'will do' surf for the rest of your life. The waves won't always be friendly. You can use your 'will do' for positive ends here – after it all it does require motivation to want to learn in the first place.

I believe we all need to feel 'can do, will do' in our lives. It brings that essential feeling of being alive that helps to smooth out the harsher elements of everyday living. The complete absence of it creates a disconnection from the life you are living, and that can be very damaging to your well-being. However, you don't and probably shouldn't have this feeling all the time. As with the first two Luck Factors, there are things in life you have to do, even if they don't engage you. Seeking perfection in everything can be as damaging as disengaging entirely.

Can do, will do – summary

- Motivation (combined with knowledge and skills) provides a very powerful force as you go through life and should be one of your aspirations.

- A lack of knowledge and skills has little to do with competence and everything to do with what you attribute your lack of knowledge to. You have immense capability.

- Be honest about gaps in your knowledge and do your best to fill in the important ones – those where the additional knowledge will maximise your impact.

- Motivation gets you a long way in life, even if at times you lack the immediate knowledge and skills required.

- The more closely you identify with what you do, the more likely you are to find yourself naturally motivated.

CHAPTER 3

Learning

'Without failure, success is not an option.'

Luck Factors in this chapter:

Luck Factor 4 – Failure is good

Luck Factor 5 – Knowing your capability

Luck Factor 6 – Being open to feedback

Luck Factor 7 – Modelling your learning

Luck Factor 8 – Turning fear into fulfilment

Learning slogans are everywhere. Your employer may have a 'learning resource centre' and talk about the 'learning culture' they are trying to develop. National governments and employers too talk about 'lifelong learning'. We have 'learning experiences' and 'development opportunities'.

All good of course, but your learning is way too important to be wrapped up in a bundle of corporate or governmental buzz words. And it's way too important to be left to the whim of others to provide it for you in formalised settings. It's something that happens every day. In fact for most of every day.

The degree to which you learn is entirely dependent on your attitude to life. A good start is to have a sense of humility so that you can admit that you don't know everything (Luck Factor 5). A willingness to evaluate setbacks and failure in a way that builds confidence is a very good second step (Luck Factor 4). The way you respond to feedback when what is said has come as a surprise to you (Luck Factor 6) and from whom you seek knowledge and inspiration (Luck Factor 7) continue the learning process.

But where it really starts is how you play out your life experiences in your head. It is, as was said in the introduction to this book, about the conversation you have with yourself about yourself. Examples of how these conversations can play out are included in this chapter, together with a walk-through of how you can turn the anxiety of a forthcoming activity or event into something you look forward to through the right kind of conversation (Luck Factor 8). The focus of this chapter is on the way you can adjust your thinking and the subsequent self-conversation. Often these are only small adjustments but they allow you to have far greater control over your own learning. There is more than a small part of me that thinks this might be the most important chapter in the book.

LUCK FACTOR 4 – FAILURE IS GOOD

'I have learned about relative failure. I saw a third place in the World Championships in 1994 as 'hideous'. But in hindsight it helped me realise that I can't always win. I have to deal with losing. A few years on, coming fourth at the Sydney Olympics was a life experience rather than a devastating loss. I immediately felt the need to prove that I was a good rower so I carried on for a while, but I also needed to prove that, although I was good at rowing, there were other things I could be good at too. So I joined a yachting team that took part in the America's Cup for a year.' GREG

In his book *Talent is Overrated*, Geoff Colvin talks of Olympic ice-dancing champion Shizuka Arakawa who is estimated to have failed 20,000 times to perform a particular dancing move in practice before she succeeded. The key here was her positive response to regular failure and the ability to absorb the pain and monotony (but perhaps it was not painful and monotonous to her?) of never-ending practice to get it right. (See the next chapter on 'Performance' for more on the value of practice.)

You might be reacting to Arakawa's persistence with amazement, but you have done the same yourself. Just look at a child learning to walk or ride a bike. Or think about when you have persisted yourself in the past to achieve something that was important to you. Learning to walk, ride a bike, drive a car or read have all required a degree of application combined with an exploratory desire that put you in the right frame of mind to succeed. There are two primary reasons why you succeeded:

- Your desire to succeed overrode any negative views you may have had about your own level of ability. (Of course, you may not have had any doubts about your ability.)

- Your explanation of the reasons for setback and failure allowed you to identify the factors that would turn failure into success.

Perhaps the biggest corrupter in the development of a success-based approach is the neutering effect of an assumption that all this success and failure come from your own genetic inheritance. Actually, if you think this then I agree with you. It's the perfect self-fulfilling statement – if you rely on genes and talent rather than your own effort, then it will be genes and talent that get you by.

If you want to perform well at anything you will encounter disappointment and failure along the way. Sometimes the success comes first and then the setbacks. Sometimes it's the other way round. It's how you explain the ebb and flow of success and failure in your own mind that determines how you act in response to them. This 'explanation' – the conversation you have with yourself about yourself – is what we call your 'explanatory style'.

Explaining setbacks and failure

We all succeed in many things in life (though it may not always feel like that). If you attribute success to 'I just got lucky' or 'Anyone can do this' you immediately negate any personal reasons for success, such as 'I worked really hard at that' or 'My hard work was rewarded'.

Imagine, for example, that you have to make a presentation about which you are nervous. You wisely enlist some help from a colleague/coach who spends time with you to get it right. You deliver a well-received presentation. You then examine the reasons for that success. A negative response may be to say 'Well, I only succeeded because I had someone helping me'. In this statement there is no acknowledgement of 'you' and your own input into the successful presentation. The positive response would be to say 'I succeeded because I enlisted help and I was prepared to listen to the advice and excellent suggestions of my coach/ colleague'. In this statement you have also identified two clear actions that you undertook, which worked for you and which will work for you again:

- It's a good idea to enlist help when I need it.
- It's a good idea to be prepared to listen to the suggestions and advice of others (even if I decide not to take up that advice).

As you read this you may be nodding your head in agreement. It all sounds so logical – and indeed it is. But this explanatory style is so central to the Luck Habit that I would like to suggest that it is worth taking a break from reading now and to reflect on some of the successes and failures you have had in life. Try to recall some of the thought processes you went through as you met with setbacks.

- How did you account for the setbacks?
- How did you account for your success?

To keep with the presentation example (because it is so common), let us look at how a person with a negative explanatory style might account for a presentation that didn't go down well. We all know what kinds of things can go wrong when you give a presentation – you lose your place, the equipment stops working, you get asked an 'impossible' question or you are just so nervous that the words don't come out as planned. Here is an example of how someone with a negative, passive explanatory style will talk this through in their own mind:

> *'I realise I am not good at presentations. In fact I'm pretty hopeless. You're either born with the "gift of the gab" or you're not. And I'm not. I get really nervous – not that that's important of course. And I didn't know that person was going to ask that question. I didn't have a clue what to say. And when the projector conked out – I wanted the ground to swallow me up. I never want to go through that again.'*

Not much scope here for a plan to have a better experience next time. There's fatalism ('I'm pretty hopeless'; 'You're either born with the "gift of the gab" or not'), not treating your needs as important ('I get really nervous – not that that's important of course') and an understandable unwillingness to have another go ('I never want to go through that again').

So let's look at this again and see how the person with a positive explanatory style might give the following responses to each of these negative experiences:

I lost my place. 'I am not the first and I won't be the last. The important thing is not to panic but to have a plan: It is perfectly OK to say to the group *"Sorry, I just got a bit lost in my notes, just give me a second to get back to where I was"*. Someone once told me that silence from a speaker's perspective seems a lot longer than it does from an audience's perspective. Perhaps I was worrying a bit too much about the silence when I was trying to find my place when actually the audience appreciated the breathing space. If I look comfortable with the silence the audience will be.

When people get lost it can mean they aren't prepared enough, so if I practised a bit more next time the sequence of my presentation would be clearer in my head. I need to give a bit more time to this.'

The AV equipment stopped working. 'This can always happen so I shouldn't chastise myself, but are there things I can do to reduce the possibility that it happens again? Check the equipment better beforehand; have back-up; check if there is an expert available and most importantly don't panic.

What can my contingency be? Have a break; have a question up my sleeve that the audience can work on in groups while I sort things out; would I be better off without the hundreds of PowerPoint slides anyway?'

The tough question. 'That was a tough question and I didn't handle it too well. I panicked a bit because I didn't have an answer. So I need to be better prepared if this does happen again. The alternatives?

Ask for responses round the room ("*Has anyone here experienced this?*") – if no-one replies, perhaps the question is too oblique anyway; admit I don't know ("*That's a very good question. I would need time to think about a response. I'll get back to you*") – a little bit of flattery makes the questioner feel good about the question they have asked too!; I could divide the room into small groups to address the question if it's important ("*That's such an important question that I feel it warrants us all taking a bit of time out to address it*").'

Nervousness. 'It's OK to be nervous, lots of people are, so what can I do to address my pre-presentation nerves? If I practise more beforehand then I can build my confidence up; perhaps I can do some breathing exercises to relax me beforehand?; I can make a conscious effort to get my first few words out extra loud and clear so that no-one picks up my nervousness and I get my voice working properly right away; slowing down can help me get control of myself; pause a bit – remembering that what seems like ages to a speaker is only a second or two for the audience.'

Responding to setbacks

Another way to look at this is to have a balanced and positive view of setbacks and their inevitability. In some situations the following responses can work for you:

Just because someone else is good doesn't mean I'm bad

Talking briefly with rower Greg Searle after he and his crew had secured silver at the 2011 World Championships, his first comment was 'We've already identified some adjustments we can make for next time'. He was complimentary too about the winners, Germany. It wasn't that his crew was not good enough. It was that the winners were very, very good. That's OK. Acknowledge excellence when you see it and use it as a spur to improve yourself. Excellence in others doesn't mean you can't be good too.

I did some really good things there

A second possible response to a big setback comes from an anecdote from Michele when looking back on the closure of her business Recycle IT and the events that led to it:

> '*I had been running a business, Recycle-IT!, which pro-vided computers for those who could not otherwise have afforded them. We provided employment for the disadvantaged and disabled – people who probably just would not have had jobs without us – and for ten years it went very well. I loved it. And then in the space of three weeks two things happened. We were cheated out of a large sum of money. And just a few days later we had to quit the space we were occupying because the com-pany that owned it (and they had been great to us) were*

expanding. Almost overnight we had to close. I felt like I was letting people down. I cried all the way through when I had to tell the team we were going to have to stop. When I looked back I learned to see what we did in another way. What I'd done was to keep a very difficult business going for ten years. We were trailblazers for computer recycling and although others were doing similar things we were inventors. We kept people in work who would not have had a job otherwise. That perspective helped me to deal with it. Looking back, I am very proud of what we did.'

This is a fabulous example of the power of positive thinking. Not only did Michele look for the positive in a difficult situation, she also found a life-affirming perspective about something that could have finished her career if she had allowed it to destroy her confidence and her belief in what she was doing.

Adam addresses the same theme in more general terms:

'Very rarely is something a complete flop. I'm trying to avoid cliché territory here, but there is usually something good in everything and I do look for that. In any project in my field, like many others, there is no 100 per cent way of knowing if it will be a success or not. Often you have to try and see. If you never have anything go wrong, you're not pushing the boundaries enough. And it's an obvious point but an important one – you have to learn from the ones that don't quite work. As a wiser person said, the only really stupid mistakes are the ones you don't learn from.

I do have things that sting from the past but you just have to let go. That can take a while – you can get the odd flashback, but there's no good dwelling on it. If you operate in an environment where experimentation is a part of what you do (it's written into Channel 4's remit and DNA), you have to accept that there will be disappointments by the very nature of the enterprise.'

Failure is good – summary

- Setback and failure is a natural, healthy part of life, not a reason to destroy confidence.

- Your response to success, setback and failure will be based on how you explain these things to yourself.

- Sometimes things happen over which you have no control. Identify the things over which you have control.

- If you succeeded, identify what you personally did to engineer that success.

- If you failed, identify what you could personally do to succeed next time.

LUCK FACTOR 5 – KNOWING YOUR CAPABILITY

This is a classic exercise originally conceived by educationalist and creativity writer Mark Brown, which I have developed. Just follow the simple instructions.

YOUR CAPABILITIES

1 *Write down a minimum of five things of which you are capable.*

You can choose from any aspect of your life. From 'work' you might choose: managing a project team, delivering a dynamic presentation or designing detailed Excel spread sheets. From 'hobbies' you might choose: playing the piano to Grade-6 level, running a mile in five minutes, building matchstick models or swimming 200 lengths of a pool without stopping. From 'home' you might choose: garden design, making a successful chocolate fondant (viewers of the BBC TV show *Masterchef* will know just how difficult this is and how much practice it takes to be perfect), designing and building your own house. Your choice is limitless and you should not, in any way, feel limited by the list here.

Think about this for a few minutes and please do not read the next instruction until you have written your list (to avoid 'contamination' in your thinking). When you are happy with your list, read on for the next instruction:

2 *Place a letter P by those that are 'proven', i.e. 'I have done this'.*

When you have done this (and only when you have done this), move on to the next instruction:

3 *Put the letter U by those which are 'unproven', i.e. 'I have not done this'.*

A majority of readers (my experiences suggest over 80 per cent) are likely to have a list of proven capabilities. Your rationale (if you were one of the 80 per cent) behind this is likely to be that you can't see this question any other way – I asked about capability and you selected a list of achievements, hobbies and perhaps even routine day-to-day things associated with domestic or working life and based your list around those.

Around 10 per cent are likely to have a list that mixes Ps and Us. The Us may be things you started – perhaps a hobby that you have taken up recently with no sense of where you might go with it or things that you were good at when you were younger and which you have half a mind to return to at some future point. In other words, a reference point from your past or present is suggesting a route for future development.

The point here is that I am not asking you to choose previously performed, provable capabilities, although you may have interpreted the question that way. What we are doing is testing how you view the word 'capability'. If you see the word 'capability' as only a personal history lesson, you may be creating a psychological barrier for yourself in the future.

As we get older many of us start to see our capabilities in terms of what we have done, rather than what we could do. This is important, as your capability list is likely to include confidence-building 'successes'. However, this mindset can be seriously limiting when you want to improve performance and seek new avenues for future opportunities for success ...

So if you are one of the 80 per cent, go back and try the exercise again, but this time think about things you have done, things you are doing and things you could do – the past, present and the future. I'm pretty sure that some things will pop out that will make you feel rather excited about your future capabilities.

Ask a 14-year-old child what they are capable of and you are likely to get a list of ambitions and desires – although on the odd occasion that I have had the chance to ask this question to younger groups you can get the opposite reaction: no list at all, as though the question is beyond the scope of the child's thinking. As we reach our twenties, reality hits (going out to work, etc.) and those ambitions and dreams get scaled down or disappear completely. That is understandable, and indeed even though it is good to have a great list of things you want to do in the future, fulfilment in any of them probably means focusing on one or two of them.

If we return to the original question – the list of your capabilities – it is important to hold on to some of those dreams and aspirations, and to ask yourself 'What capabilities have I yet to develop?' These could be reflected in things you currently do but want to get better at, or in things that you have thought about doing but haven't yet started. You might look at returning to things that captured you in your youth that have been put on the backburner since then. The cliché that says 'The only limit on your capability is what you believe the extent of that capability to be' may, like many clichés, have more than a small element of truth in it.

Knowing your capability – summary

- See your capabilities not just in terms of what you have done, but what you *could* do.

- Be open-minded about the things you could try.

- Be open-minded about how good you could become at the things you try.

- Ask yourself, too, about the things that engaged you in the past, which you've almost forgotten about, but with which you could reawaken your interest – it is good to go back sometimes.

- Remember that your capabilities are infinite.

LUCK FACTOR 6 – BEING OPEN TO FEEDBACK

The way you receive feedback – particularly criticism – is essential to the growth of the Luck Habit. There is something formative and primal about the way we receive it, in particular our reaction to it, which goes back to our earliest memories. You were given feedback by parents, relatives, childminders and so on. You went through education and got lots of it. And then on to work where, if you work in conventional environments, it continues to be given from the first day through to retirement – formally in appraisal interviews and informally on an ad hoc basis from colleagues and managers. If you play sport or take part in other kinds of hobbies and leisure pursuits, you probably get lots of it too.

In those formative years we were all affected by feedback in different ways. Some of us have taken feedback as a means of reinforcing declining confidence levels (particularly if it was given during our teenage years, when our hormones were all over the place) and the effects may have been very damaging and long lasting.

If you see criticism as meaning 'I am no good' you will probably react emotionally when you receive it (if only on the inside). This is particularly true if the giver draws attention to something we were aware of but didn't know anybody else had noticed; or if the giver tells us something we were completely unaware of.

I know many people whose confidence levels are much lower than their capability warrants and we can only guess at what events had created that. You may be one of those people yourself. It is easy to let feedback affect you in this way for the rest of your life.

But criticism can be a powerful friend, and instead of meaning you are irretrievably bad at something, it can instead mean 'I can be good'. Top performers have learned to see feedback as a way to identify ways to improve their performance and to use it as a springboard to take them forward.

One common theme among our interviewees was that, unprompted in most cases, there were critical moments where feedback was received that could have pushed them back a long way and even forced them to give up what they were doing. An example from Mo features at the end of this section. As you read Jonathan's experience below, think how you might have reacted in the same situation.

'A really important moment for me came when about six months after I had taken on a new role as head of HR for a global corporate practice in a law firm and got some feedback. My predecessor was excellent and had had a good relationship with the lawyers. I thought I had made a good start but the feedback I got was "He tries". That was it. It was a low moment in my career – I was telling myself "You're not doing well and you think you are".

In any job I think it is important to ask "What do they want from me. What should I be doing?" So, although I was shaken by the feedback, I decided that the best thing I could do was to seek advice from those self-same lawyers. When I probed the response I got was: "We didn't mean it like that. We didn't want you to get too comfortable. We wanted to keep you on your toes."

It became a model for me on how to give feedback – or rather on how not to give feedback! But it also taught me to be proactive in getting to the underlying reasons why feedback had been given in the way it was – to explore a bit more. I could have carried that "low moment" with me for a long time.' JONATHAN

An essential element in your own improvement is your willingness to receive feedback. This can be tough. We receive feedback all the time but we often find it too personal ('You're not tough enough'), poorly timed (in the middle of a crisis for example), vague ('You're not very good at making presentations are you?') and one-directional. That is to say, you have little opportunity for input in the conversation. Sometimes feedback is given during the set piece of the appraisal interview (a process often driven by other departments and not the two people involved), with neither party showing much enthusiasm for it. Sometimes it feels personal, as though the giver is having a dig at your personality.

However, the upside is that there are many things you can do to manoeuvre a feedback conversation into a tool to help you to improve your own performance. You cannot always choose how and when feedback is given to you, but you can choose how you respond to it. Your first step is to address the mindset you have about the whole idea of receiving feedback. These are common mindsets that create a barrier to the positive reception of feedback:

- **Bad feedback is my fault**. If you feel bad about yourself after feedback has been given (loss of confidence, for example) or if you have had bad experiences with feedback in the past, it can be because the feedback has been badly given. A good feedback giver will turn a potentially difficult conversation into a positive experience for you because they understand the importance of identifying positive, remedying action.

- **Feedback is always fact**. It isn't. In many circumstances it is one person's (or group's) opinion. Of course that opinion may be right, but it is for you to decide if you agree with it or not.

- **Feedback means criticism**. It can do. It can also mean praise. But so what? Welcome it rather than be on the defensive. It could be a great chance to do something better rather than a means of reducing confidence further.

■ **Feedback means permanent inadequacy**. It doesn't. All it means at the moment it is given is that you don't know how to do something properly or, if you do, you aren't applying that knowledge in the right way. The feedback can be the means by which you then seek the answers.

I cannot emphasise enough how important it is that you take a positive approach to receiving feedback regardless of how badly or inappropriately it is given (because it often will be) or whether your gut reaction is to agree or disagree. Your gut reaction and your subsequent, more considered reaction, may be very different. My approach is designed to make you an active part of the conversation, rather than a passive observer of comments being made about you.

Feedback is opportunity

Feedback is an opportunity. What matters now is that you use it as such. The recommendations below on receiving feedback are based on you taking control – both of the situation and of your reaction to it.

■ **Ask for specific examples**. Feedback is often given in general terms. A comment such as 'You sometimes let people dominate you in meetings' is not a lot of use to you (particularly if you are unaware of your behaviour) unless it is supported by a specific example. Feedback given as a generalisation is useless because you have no specific experience to relate it to, so ask for specifics. You could say something like: 'Can you tell me when I did this?' or 'How did I do this?'

- **Consider what the effects will be**. A good coach or manager will say 'When you did x, y happened'. However, you may need to prompt the feedback giver or consider the consequences yourself.

- **Thank the feedback giver**. Do not engage in an argument, otherwise they are unlikely to give you feedback again. Say something like, 'Thank you for that, I haven't thought about it before. I need time to go away and think about what to do next.' This leaves the giver feeling you having received the feedback positively and that you recognise the need to consider what has been said.

- **Decide what course of action to take but don't rush your decision making**. In a formal workplace situation we can feel under pressure to immediately commit to something. Don't. You need time to consider what has been said and allow yourself the space to resolve any emotional response you've had to the feedback. In Mo Nazam's example below, too much emotional contamination could have blocked good judgement, but he managed to pull himself back from what could have been a damaging reaction. Then you can decide on your course of action. Remember that while you of course have the right to disagree with what has been said and to decide not to act on it, make sure you have considered it carefully before you do so. Ask yourself: 'Was I aware of this?'; 'Has someone else said something similar?'; 'Do they have a point?'

I became close friends with a brilliant guitar player named Phil Hillborne. We would talk for hours on the phone about guitar players and playing, and we'd swap recordings and generally feed each other's passion for *playing. He used to demo guitars at trade shows and once, when I was playing one of the guitars, he said: "You're a really good player, Mo, but your vibrato is ****". He was right.*

Your vibrato is the trademark of your guitar personality and a good vibrato can help you sound more individual. I could have thrown my toys out of the pram, but instead I worked very hard to improve my vibrato over the next year or so. I developed exercises, watched videos of great players like Peter Green and listened to how singers (particularly Aretha Franklin) used vibrato. I practised it every day and really worked on the subtle movements of wrist and fingers that are needed to really control the vibrato. Years later I was in a shop trying out a guitar and there was an elderly man sitting there, just hanging out. I gave the guitar back to the shop assistant and as I walked out the elderly man tapped me on the shoulder and said "You've got a nice vibrato, son". The hard work paid off. MO

Accepting praise

In my experience those who find it difficult to take criticism also find it difficult to accept praise. Some people are embarrassed when they get praise. Praise is also feedback, but some of the rules for criticism above may not be so easily applicable here. With praise it may be hard to ask for a specific example without being seen to solicit positive comments about yourself ('Wasn't I brilliant? Now tell me why'). Assuming you feel the praise was sincere – too many managers, for example, give praise as a throwaway remark because they think it is the right thing to do – you may find it valuable to look at the good things you did. Lots of effort, lots of practice, enjoyable task, something different? All might be the reasons why you performed well. This analysis may give you a useful window into your own self and what it is that makes something enjoyable for you. Enjoyment usually leads to performance improvement.

Here is an example from Jonathan when he received feedback – effectively praise – very early in his career, when he was leaving a role that was particularly difficult:

'I was PA to the director of corporate affairs for 18 months. It was a very stressful role as he was chronically dis-organised and inefficient, although he was loved by many for his great charisma and charm. I felt that people would hold me to account for his inefficiency but, although they gave me a hard time while I was in the role, the feedback at the end from colleagues was that I had done as well as anyone could to move things on, despite his obvious disorganisation. The feedback helped me to learn a few important lessons. It gave me an early experience of what I call the "big beasts" – those big egos that tend to run the show – so I could see what they were really like and get used to dealing with them. It also made me see that people will under-stand the environment in which you are operating and make some allowance for it. I realised that charisma may get you the job, but you need a level of efficiency and delivery if you are going to keep the job (which the director of corporate affairs did not). In my work now, whenever it gets tough I think back to that role and life never seems so bad now since, no matter how much pressure there is, I am (mostly) in control.' JONATHAN

This makes the point about being specific once again. The feedback must have been good if it gives you praise. It gives you a nice feeling. But it becomes infinitely more valuable if you are able to be specific about what you did to make you successful.

Honest self-appraisal

Receiving feedback from others does not preclude self-critique. As we have seen above, self-critique can be catalysed by feedback from others. However, you should not wait for this. Just as persistence can allow you to develop good habits leading to better performance, you can also develop bad habits, as many sportspeople can attest, unless you are able to challenge what you are doing in a constructive manner. This does not mean paralysing yourself through over-analysis. But it does mean a regular, honest self-appraisal.

Being open to feedback – summary

- See feedback conversations as something you are centrally part of, rather than something that happens to you.

- Use feedback, no matter how badly it is given, as an opportunity to improve – because you can – rather than as a reason to lower your confidence.

- Relate feedback to a specific experience and ask yourself how you would do it differently/better next time.

- Criticism can also be praise. The best feedback is often a mix of what you did well and what can be improved.

- Without feedback you stand still. Welcome feedback – even if the feedback may not be what you were expecting.

LUCK FACTOR 7 – MODELLING YOUR LEARNING

'If that's what the best do, then I am an idiot for not taking their advice.' MO

Up to the age of 20 you may have been forced to perform in environments where others – perhaps almost everyone – seemed better than you in academic or sporting challenges. In school sports you may have been acutely aware of this if you were one of the last to be chosen in a sports team after the best players had been shared between the two team captains. Or perhaps in mathematics there always seemed to be a 'boffin' in the subject who made you very aware that you were not one. At worst this can be a humiliating experience.

At school perhaps you were not able to choose your arenas of performance and so you then resolved to 'find your own place'. Maybe you assumed that this place was among people of the same perceived levels of ability to yourself (the word 'perceived' is key here). To give the very best performance you are capable of, it is important to 'unlearn' this negative mindset. We often rationalise our capability levels in the following way: 'John is brilliant at mathematics because he is very intelligent. I am not brilliant at maths and therefore I am not very intelligent.'

There are two things to consider here:

- There is always the 'one best'. But this person is only the 'one best' at that moment.

■ What does it matter anyway? For all but the most hyper-competitive, it is much more useful to think in terms of being the best you can be (which could be almost limitless).

Instead of living in this damaging mindset, you may find it more valuable to ask what you can learn from the best. You want to get better at tennis? Play against players who are better than you. The areas where you need to improve most will be magnified because your opponent will find them for you. These vulnerabilities may be hidden against lesser players because they won't find them. And against better players you will get more opportunities to strengthen those vulnerabilities because you will get lots of practice. In the same way, if you want to be a better presenter at team meetings, watch someone who does it well and make a note of what they do that helps them be good. And then practise.

The point is that you can choose to see the success and achievements of others as something that amplifies what you *perceive* to be your lesser achievements or ability. *Or* you can use their achievements as your own spur.

This 'modelling' comes in two forms and combines two things that appear regularly in this book – the head and the heart. To appeal to the heart, inspiration from others can be sought – someone has done this, has shown what's possible. To appeal to the head you need to know the practical tools that will help you to improve. This combination of the inspirational and practical provides a very powerful dynamic that can fuel your own development.

Inspiration – what's possible?

'When I was 12 years old Martin Cross came in to talk to the school. Martin had just won a rowing gold medal at the '84 Olympics. It made a big impression. Someone made something possible. I just thought "Here's an ordinary guy who did an extraordinary thing". He made the best of what he had. It's not about heroic figures for me, but role models are very important.' GREG

Pioneers are able to demonstrate the art of the possible. They do things that haven't been achieved before. That's one kind of inspirational figure. Another kind do things that have been done, but do it in such a way that it resonates with you – through force of personality, with humour, or with an idiosyncratic approach.

Greg got his role model at school although he's clear that, for him, the heroic, inspirational figure is not so important. In fact lots of us get role models and inspirational figures at school. The teacher you remember best may not be remembered for anything in particular they said, but for a feeling they stirred in you that history or books or science or sport or music could be interesting.

This is not just an age/school thing. A friend of mine, Helene, started singing lessons at the age of 67 and has ended up in the London Philharmonic Choir travelling all over the world. When I tell this story to audiences I can feel a huge sense of the art of the possible suddenly entering the room. I'm sure you can think of someone in your life who has done something that inspires you.

It's tough to write about sources of inspiration because it's just so unique and personal to each of us, but here are three things to think about:

- Helene wasn't 'lucky'. Nor was Greg Searle or Martin Cross. They did many things to create luck. When you look a bit deeper at those who seem to have all the luck, it was because they took some very specific actions to kick-start the whole process – they were active players in their own lives rather than passives waiting for the luck to happen to them. If you think people create much of their luck then you have taken a step in using the success of others to create an inspirational base for yourself.

- Inspiration often comes from those who maintain deeply held values and live through them, for example, Nelson Mandela or Aung San Suu Kyi. As I suggested in Luck Factor 1, your values provide a strong compass, moral or otherwise, for the direction you choose to take. Taking inspiration from almost seemingly untouchable figures can help because they again show what's possible.

- It does help not to paint inspirational figures into gods. As someone once said: 'Never meet your heroes!' You're not necessarily using their whole life as an inspirational base, but rather what they specifically do. We all have vulnerabilities, so do cut them some slack – whether they are role models or heroes.

Practical tools

'I went to lots of gigs and made a conscious effort to see the very best. I noticed even then that some of my contemporaries were giving up. They would say "I am never

going to be that good, I give up". I would say "No, I want to be like that" and I would go off and practise. I would constantly model my learning on what the best could do.' MO

The practical element to modelling means using your head to identify the specific actions you need to take to develop your knowledge and skills. This might come formally when being coached or mentored, for example, or less formally through your own observations of others. Here are some tips:

- A willingness to learn from others always starts with a self-admission of your own vulnerability:
  - 'I don't know this and I need to.'
  - 'I don't and can't know everything.'
  - 'That didn't go well, I need to be honest and admit I just don't know how to do it.'

  (There is more of this admission of vulnerability at the end of this section.)
- You also need to build on success:
  - 'Right, I have got so far by myself, I now need to start looking more at what others do.'
  - 'That went really well, the next step is to take some lessons.'
- Listen to what's said with an open mind. You are not necessarily seeking the perfect piece of advice to copy – you are getting insight from someone else who has experienced similar things to you.

- Pay attention to feelings. Don't just look at the specific things role models do, but look at the way they express the feelings they have about the problems they have had:
  - 'This can be very frustrating.'
  - 'It took me hours to get this bit right.'
  - 'It just didn't feel natural at first.'

  Sometimes it's just good to know that you are not the only person in the world who has your challenges.

- Sometimes role models plant seeds rather than hand over the mighty oak. Learn to nurture the seed – and create your version of their mighty oak. It will be different.

- If you are learning through observation or through formal coaching, take the chance to practise what you have seen as soon as you can afterwards. This reinforces learning. In more formal settings trainers say that up to 80 per cent of learning is lost within seven days if course participants don't reinforce the learning themselves.

- If you are being formally coached, you need to understand the style of your coach. Some like the spark of more heated discussion – the throwing back and forth of ideas – while others prefer the opposite. Learn to adapt.

- When you are being formally coached, be an active part of the coaching session – ask questions and say how you feel:
  - 'I found this bit tough.'
  - 'Can you show me that again?'
  - 'I'm struggling to get the hang of this.'

■ Show humility in your source of inspiration and learning. Musician Neil Young acknowledges how much he learnt from Scottish folk musician Bert Jansch, just by listening to the way he plucks the chords and his guitar 'styling'. In fact he still learns from him now, 40 years on. (You probably haven't heard of Bert Jansch, who died in 2011. He had a relatively uncommercial sound that rewards patient, persistent listening.) This is a great example of an internationally renowned musician seeking out interesting and challenging places and people and being open-minded enough to see how they can help develop their own skills. Performance improvement never stops and neither does the search from whom and from where we can develop our own skills. If you see someone doing something well, ask yourself, 'What do they do that I don't do or know how to do?' It doesn't matter who they are.

■ Remember: role models – yes; intimidation – no. There is a subtle difference between 'modelling' and blindly following. Writer and social commentator J.B. Priestley, in a long-forgotten but excellent book *Over The Long High Wall*, reminded us that too often we find ourselves, as he puts it: 'Submitting to the rules of the ambitious (whose motivation is themselves) rather than the rules of the wise.' Politics is an obvious example of this, but it is also common in professional life. Indeed, no matter what environment it is in which you operate, you have probably come across these ambitious types. Sometimes you have to play musical chairs a little to keep them at bay. But don't play their tune.

'I don't know this'

In this Luck Factor I suggested that to be honest with yourself and others about your lack of knowledge and skills is healthy. But for many of us it can be hard to admit 'I don't know this'. Some people rationalise this as showing weakness. In fact, to me, this admission is a higher form of intelligence. It's great when I hear the words 'Can you show me how to do this?' instead of watching someone trying to bluff their way through something they clearly know nothing about.

Ignorance is a permanent condition. But not knowing something is simply a temporary gap in knowledge, which can be filled at any time if you want to. A good example of this is technology. Whether it's eBooks, a new mobile phone, apps, social networking or the latest advancement in tablets, you can be left feeling like you are behind the curve, grasping for knowledge and breathless in the pursuit to keep up to date. And yet we do catch up, but some of us do it more easily and faster than others. These people have a mindset of: 'It's important I know this. I need to observe what others do. I need to ask others to show me how to do things. I need to investigate how to gain this knowledge. I need to read a book on it or go on a course.'

Clearly some of us do this and some of us don't. If you are one of the 'don'ts' it can help to understand the reasons why – the blocks:

- **Stubbornness**. This can be a real strength or a vulnerability. It can be great when it's about defending strongly held values. But it's seriously limiting when it's because people do not want to have to think anymore. Stubbornness – often expressed as a rejection of anything new – provides a convenient veil.

- **I am intelligent**. Therefore I am right! The people with the highest assessment of their own intelligence (intelligence is 'subjective' in my view, especially given how many forms of it there are) can rationalise themselves out of further learning. This can mean dismissing what doesn't fit their view of the world and only letting in what reinforces it. It's a bit like the way in which some people only read one newspaper (and strictly only 'one') – the one whose political stance they agree with.

- **Lack of confidence**. Often this is expressed in its most damaging form as them versus me, i.e. everyone knows more than me. If you sometimes get this feeling about yourself, you may find that it goes back to education when, for example, a stand-out pupil transcended what everyone else did. Or you just didn't perform as well as a few others. But perhaps the environment wasn't right for you (and the formal process of learning at school isn't right for a lot of people), or you needed to pace yourself (speed of learning has little to do with capacity for learning) or the things you were really interested in weren't the things tested (artistic ability for example, which is rarely on the priority list of subjects at school, is suddenly much-prized as our world has become hyper-visual, graphic and screen-based).

- **My world is your world**. There is a very powerful voice inside us that wants to tell everyone how much we know. There are many reasons for this, but one of them is that we think the other person will be impressed by all this knowledge. But the really smart thing to do is to use this the other way. People like to talk about themselves and they really like people who give them a chance to do so. So, in dialogue, try turning things round:

  - 'That's an interesting perspective, what made you see things that way?'
  - 'I hadn't thought of it like that – tell me more.'
  - 'What was your experience of that?'
  - 'How did this make you see things differently?'

Modelling your learning – summary

- The hardest thing for some people is to say 'I don't know'. Be honest with yourself about what you don't know (see Luck Factor 8).

- If you ever think 'I can't do that' there is usually someone who has shown what can be done – and even if there isn't, someone has to be first.

- If you model yourself on others you need to engage both your heart and your head. The heart provides the propulsion, the head the essential actions.

- Actively listen and observe.

- Reinforce and practise.

LUCK FACTOR 8 – TURNING FEAR INTO FULFILMENT

A mistake or a single bad experience can take on an importance out of all proportion to its original context. If you allow the pressure to build around the idea that you must avoid making the same or a similar mistake in the future you create a pressure around that situation, which makes it more likely that you will repeat it. Earlier in this chapter I used making a presentation as an example illustrating how to respond to failure. We can use that example again here. Say you have a bad experience for some of the reasons presented previously – perhaps you found it tough to answer some of the difficult questions. If you don't address the issue afterwards then that tough situation gets translated into fear of its reoccurrence and/or avoidance of the situation where it could occur again.

How does this fear manifest itself in practice? You find yourself making a presentation and you get to the bit when you ask for questions. Instead of a confident invitation to the audience such as: 'I have raised some important points here that I know directly affect the work you are doing and I also know that some of you will want to ask me some questions' … your voice will be timid and less confident, your body language defensive (perhaps even one of your arms will be placed across your body or covering part of your face, and you will show no or little hand movement). The words you actually use will be passive: 'Does anybody have any questions?' You've transmitted your fear to the group through your tone, words and body language, and the group expresses a collective but silent 'no'.

SID and apprehension

In the introduction to this book I referred to what is known as your inner dialogue, and – in the case of a positive conversation with yourself – your SID or 'sound inner dialogue'. Your inner dialogue refers to a conversation that you have with yourself and could be either one of these two alternatives:

- **A reference to the past** where you try to explain what has happened to you and why it has happened. You may, for example, find it difficult to circulate and make conversation in social situations such as parties and you found yourself leaving last night's party early because you felt awkward (or you got really drunk as a way to try to deal with it). Or perhaps you play a team sport and your team has just lost badly and you are trying to work out why. (We covered this earlier in the chapter when we looked at accounting for success or failure.)

- **When you look to the future** and have a conversation with yourself about how you think a particular situation will unfold. For example, you may have to have a potentially difficult conversation with a friend about something that has irritated you. Perhaps you had agreed to meet somewhere and the other person hadn't turned up and you want to ask them why. Or you have an important presentation to deliver and the last one didn't go so well.

In the examples I have used I have referred to things that haven't gone well or the anticipation of something that might not. This inner dialogue refers equally to things that have gone well or impending situations that you feel confident about.

We all have these conversations – the inner dialogue – all the time and they can be paralysing or liberating. In this final section I want to look at how you overcome the anxiety or even fear of dealing with a particular impending situation that you do not feel comfortable about – what is called your anticipatory anxiety. How can you turn this fear into a positive force?

Here is a technique (adapted from psychologist Martin Seligman's ABCDE method) to address negative or excessively pessimistic thinking in order not to let those thoughts control you. The technique goes one step further because it also moves you to an optimistic frame of mind about what you had previously felt uncomfortable about.

The process has six steps:

Step 1 – The situation (S)

Identify the difficult situation you foresee.

Step 2 – The specifics (S)

What is it specifically that you are uncomfortable with about this situation?

Step 3 – The significance (S)

It is important that you understand how your feelings about this situation impact on your behaviour. Nervous about something? What are the likely effects of those nerves?

Step 4 – The implications (I)

A dose of realism is needed. First, is the worst-case scenario likely to occur anyway? Second, you need to understand that the previously identified impact on your behaviour is likely to create the very situation you had anticipated. In other words it plays out as a self-fulfilling prophecy.

Step 5 – The investigation (I)

The investigation injects a dose of reality and flips the negative feelings into a positive frame of mind. You start with the following questions:

- 'Has this ever happened to me before?'

- 'Am I looking at the worst-case scenario and playing this as though it is likely to happen every time?'

- Many of us are prone to exaggeration – we act out a small difficulty in our minds and turn it into something more insidious. We make catch-all statements about our level of ability, i.e. 'I am no good'. So ask, 'Am I exaggerating? Which of these specific anxieties or fears are actually true or partially true?'

Having injected balance you then address the specific points you raised in step 2. Worried that the equipment won't work properly when you make a presentation? Then prepare properly and make sure the equipment is working beforehand and have a back-up plan. Worried that the opposition striker is quicker than you and will beat you to the ball every time? Then develop a strategy to deal with it – play a bit further back and take away the opposing player's space advantage. Worried that you don't have credibility in the eyes of others? Ask yourself what steps you can take to address it (assuming that there is some truth to it) – voice, dress, body language, etc. Of course this last one is a very big issue indeed and will not be resolved by a simple SID. But it will raise the issues to address from which you can make progress.

Step 6 – Dynamism (D)

Once you have investigated and come up with responses that make it less likely to become real, you may now see the 'difficult situation' as an opportunity rather than something to be feared. There is now dynamism and drive in your actions because you have challenged your fears and developed strategies for overcoming them.

The SID approach in action

In Chapter 6 ('People') we will be looking at developing your network in different ways – one-on-one and in social situations such as conferences and meetings. We will demonstrate how to use this SID approach with a specific example – dealing with the apprehension felt when networking in large group situations.

A final thought

When your desire to learn stops, you stop.

> *'I still want to get better. I have recently taken up classical guitar on a more formal basis and I am myself now a guitar tutor. It is great to be a full-time musician. But I worked very hard to become one.'* MO

Turning fear into fulfilment – summary

- Don't talk yourself into a state of fear or anxiety about minor problems.

- Avoid creating your own anticipated reality through your own negative mindset.

- You do not have a fixed level of ability. Positive conversations with yourself change you. Life is not a fait accompli.

- Bigger challenges can be overcome with a step-by-step approach to dealing with your vulnerabilities.

- It is possible to look forward to something that you previously felt uncomfortable about.

CHAPTER 4

Performing

'One thing I have noticed is that the top performers care deeply about their own performance. They keep their standards very high, and they are driven of course, but they have a willingness to be coached, which also suggests a degree of humility. There is no substitute for hard work anywhere and lawyers themselves work very, very hard. But, and it might sound obvious but it's true, some of the best ones are able to combine this hard work with a work/life balance. They have other interests.' JONATHAN

Luck Factors in this chapter:

Luck Factor 9 – Hard work

Luck Factor 10 – What's the point?

Luck Factor 11 – Thinking without thinking

Luck Factor 12 – Keeping fresh

What constitutes a 'world-class performance' is subjective. But what constitutes a 'brilliant performer' is not. If we look at the best performers – whether they operate in traditional work environments, play sport or a musical instrument or indulge in politics – there are key characteristics that almost all of them seem to share most of the time. This chapter is designed to make those characteristics understandable and accessible to you so that you can apply them in your own life. It works well with the Luck Factors introduced in Chapter 1 where we looked at the level of affinity you have with what you do.

Parts of this book are designed to help you perform at a level at which you may not have previously thought you were capable. You might work in a call centre and want to increase your sales over the phone. You might be a team leader or manager and want to develop your leadership skills. You might play the guitar as a hobby but want to improve. You might be a parent who wants to help your children express themselves to the world in a way that suits *them* best.

Over the last 20–30 years research has told us that talent is not the sole predictor of success and may not even be a reliable one. With our growing knowledge of how the brain works and how certain elements of it change and adapt with regular stimulation (like the way an arm muscle develops if you regularly lift weights with it), we can say with a degree of certainty that the gifts you were presented with at birth are helpful, but do not guarantee much in terms of performance later in life. In fact, the field of popular psychology (Geoff Colvin's *Talent is Overrated* and Matthew Syed's *Bounce* are good examples) suggests that nothing is as valuable as meaningful, purposeful practice, regardless of the talents you were born with. This purposeful practice helps you learn, develop and grow in whatever arena of life you want to, so that you can perform at an elevated level. This, combined with your intrinsic motivation – your internal desire to perform in a particular sphere – makes for a winning combination.

LUCK FACTOR 9 – HARD WORK

Hard work wins

Nigel Roberts was captain of Great Britain's over-35 ice hockey team. He continues, since retiring from the sport, to coach at his club, Hull Kingston Cobras. He has had a great chance to see how youngsters develop over time. What he has noticed is that those who came to the sport at the age of 12 or 13 and do well right away are often not those who succeed aged 18, 19 or 20. Says Nigel:

> 'What seems to happen is that those people who attribute their success to talent assume that the success curve will continue to grow for them because they are talented. The youngsters who succeed later often do so because they have had to work hard to become good. They understand how to overcome failure and disappointment because the path to the top for them has been tougher. Talent gets you so far, but hard work is the thing that really gets you to the top. I've noticed this in many other aspects of life too. What's important to me is that if you do have an aptitude for something then it is a very powerful mix if you can combine it with hard work. But to me the hard work is the thing.'

We love quick fixes. For example we all know that the best way to lose weight effectively is to eat less and exercise more. But that doesn't stop us spending billions on diets where little evidence exists for their efficacy. We want to avoid the exercise bit because it takes time and is difficult. Taking this further, a quick flick through the shadier digital channels on daytime TV reveals a huge number of fat-burning/muscle-toning devices that apparently do their work while we lie on the sofa. I am not convinced.

Performance does not come with a quick fix. Performing at your best comes with a commitment to immersion and hard work to get you to the level at which you want to perform. Winston Churchill, when asked about his apparent brilliance at public speaking 'off the top of his head' replied, 'Impromptu speeches are not worth the paper they are written on'. He spent days getting his speeches right.

I am as I am?

A really important starting point in performing well is the belief that you can and will get better. What's the point of the hard work if you don't believe this? This is not as obvious and universally believed as you or I might think. You must not simply accept that there is a predetermined, birth-defined limit on your capability. Luck Factor 5 'Knowing your capability' suggested why some of us have such a restrictive view of what we can do. In all likelihood you will only perform up to the level to which you think you are capable, although we all surprise ourselves sometimes – which should be evidence enough that there is a lot more in you than you may have thought.

Those surprise moments are worth capturing and they should not be viewed as 'beginner's luck' or some such fatalistic view. This is because the fatalistic approach does not allow for the necessary physical and psychological adaptations to be made through hard work. In fact advances in human understanding – neurological and otherwise – are starting to suggest that you can and do change if you are willing to invest time in making those changes.

Some studies have shown that certain parts of the brain do have a degree of plasticity when exposed to new stimuli. One now seminal study conducted in 2000 showed that one part of the brain's hippocampus (believed to have a responsibility for spatial awareness) in London taxi drivers was bigger than a control group and proportionally bigger in the most experienced drivers. I am not making the claim that the brain is expanding and contracting all the time depending on whatever stimuli it is exposed to at that particular time. But the evidence does seem clear that stimulation creates increased electrical activity in the appropriate part of the brain, and the brain makes, over time, the adaptations that allow you to improve. Your hard wiring – the essence of your personality – does not change. But your soft-wiring – the elements of you and your brain that are able to change with regular exposure to new patterns of thinking and behaviour – does.

This is where Luck Factor 1 is again so important. You just aren't going to push for any length of time for things for which you feel no affinity. But the results can be wondrous if you feel affinity, believe that the more you put in the more you get out, and that you can perform beyond levels you may have thought possible.

Let's have a real-life example. You may be a supervisor or manager who wants to be better at the job of managing others. You realise that you need to show more empathy with the team, understanding things from the team's point of view, rather than just telling them what to do. So you try. It might not feel natural at first but in time, through practice, your brain and the way you think adapts and those characteristics of the empathic manager become more natural to you – if you are willing to invest this time. You feel more comfortable in your new behavioural surroundings because your brain, developing through experience, makes it so.

Myelin is a fat that coats nerve endings (creating the myelin sheath) in the brain and speeds up 'connections' between different parts of the brain. Neurology is showing us that this stimulation changes our very plastic brain, allowing us to develop the parts of the brain that facilitate improvement and excellence in performance. If you want your arms to get stronger, you exercise them. In the same way it's not such a great leap to suggest that if you want to be a better manager at work by showing more empathy, you need to practise it.

Practice with purpose

'When I was about 14 I noticed an old Woolworths' electric guitar under my brother's bed. He never used it so I asked if I could borrow it. From that moment, I knew this was "me". I played for what felt like hours at a time. I even gave up playing out with my friends at school so that I could practise (there was no playground at the school anyway). I was working hard to

*catch up because I knew that a lot of good guitar play-
ers had started much younger than me. At this stage
my learning had not been formalised in any way. I took
myself off to college, where I took O levels and then A
levels, but all the time I made a point of meeting musicians and jamming with similar-minded students or
even people I met at gigs. I balanced this with my own
more free-form methods of learning. In the very early
1980s I bought copies of the American magazine* Guitar
Player *at great expense. In the back there was always
an extended feature on different aspects of technique,
which would be written by one of the great guitar players of the era – Frank Zappa, Larry Coryell or Robert
Fripp perhaps. Here I could learn the basics of things
like harmony.'* MO

Mo here talks of the immersion and hard work he needed
to get to be good. There is a huge amount of research
which suggests that, while innate talent helps, what seems
to separate the top performers from the rest is the amount
of time they are willing to invest in themselves in order to
perform – that's the hard work bit. But it is actually about
more than that. Not only is the investment time important
but there must also be a *purpose* to this investment. If you
want to find out more about this I can recommend Matthew
Syed's well-researched book *Bounce.*

Practice and the pain of repetition

Repetition can be boring. One of the ways you can test how
'intrinsically motivated' you are to do something will come
from how much pain (particularly in physical activity) you

can endure and how prepared you are to keep practising something to help you get better. One way of overcoming pain – either physical or mental – is to think about the way you will feel when you have achieved what you are practising (see 'Practice and self-actualisation' below).

I hope will you allow me to indulge in a personal example. I have been a semi-serious swimmer for two years. When I started to swim I did so to lose weight. Which I did. But I quickly realised I needed more than that. I loved swimming – I had the affinity I've said is so important – but I had to have bigger reasons to be in the water. Keeping the weight off was now not enough. So I entered a 2.5-kilometre 'swimathon' (100 lengths) and trained for it. The first time I swam 100 lengths non-stop in practice was such a fantastic feeling. So, to keep interested, I set myself a time target and hit it in the actual 'swimathon' event. As soon as I completed it I resolved to enter the following year and set a new time target (seven minutes quicker) and hit that too. At the time of writing I have taken a further ten minutes off my 2.5-kilometre time so that by the next 'swimathon' I should be around 20–22 minutes quicker than just over two years ago. Every time I get in the pool I have a purpose. It prevents boredom and the pain of repetition – going up and down a pool with no purpose can be very boring indeed. I have recently been working on reducing the proportion of breaststroke lengths in relation to freestyle lengths so that I can easily do 100 freestyle lengths with no breaststroke at all (freestyle is much quicker and more physically demanding than breaststroke). I vary it. The more I push myself in the pool, the better the feeling is when I have finished – the sense of pride, particularly if I have knocked a few seconds off my time and I also get that lovely 'high' of endorphin release that hard physical exercise gives you.

Now, this 'practice with purpose' is personal. This works for me and the kind of person I am. What will work for you and the kind of person you are may be different. But that purpose has to be there if you want to improve. Doing it step-by-step, day-by-day seems to be the way that most performers do it, while always having the big performance goal in mind. This step-by-step approach is developed further in Chapter 5 'Purpose', where specific examples are given of learning a new language and public speaking.

Practice and self-actualisation

Keeping the performance goal in mind – or self-actualisation – stimulates a heightened sense of motivation. It's what gets you through – if you can see yourself performing well in your chosen field it creates a great sense of purpose as you develop the skills that will help you achieve your high performance goals. If you can see it, but the sight is not that energising for you, then you may be wasting your time contemplating it.

Practice and requalification

One of the things that fascinates me is how much younger generations seem to know about the world when everyone seems to want to belittle educational achievement ('Exams were so much harder in my day'). Who knows? The question whether exams used to be tougher is pointless and the answers are often self-justifying. Seven- and eight-year-olds seem to know things I definitely did not know when I was their age. The point is that the knowledge that gets us so far quickly gets superseded by technological advances, people who just know more than us (which can be very hard to admit), and satisfaction at our own performance level. Good performers requalify, whatever their age, experience and previous successes. So:

- Keep abreast of new techniques and approaches – don't just dismiss them.
- Ask 'What am I still doing that's become obsolete?'
- Show a willingness to develop your skills, whatever your age or previous success (see Jonathan's quote at the beginning of this chapter).

Hard work – summary

- The best performers work hard.
- There should always be a purpose to this hard work.
- There should also always be a purpose when developing new skills.
- Use the 'future you' as a motivational tool.
- Don't get left behind through complacency.

LUCK FACTOR 10 – WHAT'S THE POINT?

In the last Luck Factor I talked about the need to create purpose when you practise – whether it's playing the guitar, swimming or improving your presentation skills. In this Luck Factor I take this idea on to an existential but no less practical level. This concerns the very reason that you choose a particular means of occupation and the role that you perform when you are 'occupied'. This might, for example, mean an accurate appraisal of what others really need from you and/or for you to be clear what it is you bring to a team or group. Perhaps the very reason that you do well in a particular sphere is that you can bring individuality to your role, but this individuality can be easily lost as you get wrapped up in day-to-day routines.

What is my role? – Being here for others

The six interviewees and countless other successful people I have worked with all share an absolute clarity about what it is they are meant to be doing in their chosen arenas of performance. Interestingly, in all cases, there is a regular reference to other people and how what these successful people do needs to relate to other people's worlds. These words from Jonathan, who works in what you might call a conventional office environment, bear this out:

'I always ask "What do they want from me?". As I provide a service for those who work with me I have to be clear about this. This changes from job to job but it is important to work this out. In my current role, for example, I need to display a reasonable degree of "intellect" – a prerequisite among lawyers. I also need to be articulate – clearly expressing my ideas but also communicating effectively. I get credibility if I can do these things. Also, the willingness to have ideas myself, and, because of the nature of the job I do, to be an enabler rather than a blocker of the ideas others have. I need to make their job easier to do.'

For Adam there are a series of filters he uses that help him, and again a key thing for him is to be able to live in other people's worlds. This is just as important in a highly creative environment as it is in an office environment:

> '*I have a number of filters which help me in my work. A big one is: "What's in it for me?" as far as the audience or user is concerned. There should be a clear benefit to them. They should be having a need met or a desire fulfilled. Another important filter is to ask: "Would I do this?" By way of illustration, I remember a number of years ago being in a meeting about commercialising broadband with a bunch of government officials and industry experts. Some of the people in the room were pushing fancy subscription models. So I asked the question: "OK, who's parted with cash to buy this kind of content online in the last six months?" (This was a few years ago.) No one had. To which the obvious reply was: "So why do you think anyone else would?"*'

(A third Adam 'filter' appears in the section later on 'Detail'.)

For Michele, the same attitude is true. She emphasises the customer in her comment:

> '*I think it's so important to put yourself in other people's shoes. I ask "What do my customers want?" (in the loosest sense of what we call "customers") and not just "This is what I do and you'd better need it". My communication style is based on this and I use it with colleagues, customers, civil servants and ministers. I want to be able to say "I've listened to you, I've heard what you need and this is how I can help".*'

So, to summarise, ask yourself what it is that other people want from you. Don't assume this – it does pay to ask if you are unsure. As Michele suggests, offering what is easiest for you may bear no relation to what is wanted. So few people seem to realise this.

What is my role? – As part of a group

Clearly an elite sportsperson has a primary role in maximising their performance in their chosen sport. However, where a sportsperson operates as part of a team, each person will need to find a role for themselves in support of the team. For Greg it means this:

> 'I encourage the team – all of them are aged between 23 and 28 – to keep perspective. We can complain about the new sets of sunglasses we have been given or other sponsor's gifts, but I remind them to keep perspective. I can act as a "bridge" between athletes and coaches pushing back to them when the situation demands it.'

So many of us operate in groups – work teams, clubs, even as a part of a family – that to be clear on what you bring to the group is important. Greg's role, given his age (40) and experience relative to his colleagues, is to use his acquired wisdom for the benefit of the team. Your performance is not finite – it has to relate to the performance of the group or team as a whole and you should evaluate what you do and how you do it in those terms.

General roles that need to be performed in groups include:

- **Leader**. This has nothing to do with being a manager. It's about having others look to you for direction because they respect you, you have a good reputation, your credibility is high or you have experience (or all of these). This role is divided into two – the 'command and tell' approach and the more collaborative, consensual method. Leaders tend to have a preference for one or the other – see Greg's quote above which suggests a combination of collaborative leader and 'harmoniser' (below).

- **Thinker**. Do you have new ideas or offer different perspectives? For example, do you enjoy playing devil's advocate? But do you always express your ideas? Sometimes the thinkers can be the quietest in a group – remember to push your ideas forward.

- **Harmoniser**. Here you provide the emotional glue for the group, repairing relationships, resolving disagreements, showing empathy and generating cohesion, perhaps even fun.

- **Doer**. Doers are action-based. They see possibilities rather than pitfalls, and generate positivity around the group.

- **Achiever/fixer**. While doers get stuff done, achievers get the right stuff done. These are often the fixers too. Fixers have a high degree of practical intelligence and are able to cut through the chaff when the group has problems.

You will not perform one of these roles to the exclusion of all others, but neither are you likely to be performing all these roles to an equal standard. My experience is that most of us perform two of these intrinsically well, a third role fairly well and the last two less well. While I am asking you to make a subjective judgement here about which role(s) sits best with you, you will find it valuable to get the honest opinions of others. But, as is suggested in many parts of this book, self-awareness is a valuable characteristic that affects many of the Luck Factors, and being open to how others see you really helps.

Why the detail?

At some point most of us get tired of what we are doing and stop or accept that 95 per cent is good enough. High achievers stick at it, finding that last little bit that turns something good into something great. I believe strongly that this extra few per cent in effort is what separates the moderate performer from the really good one. Greg Searle talks about the extra little bit he gives in training, and its significance:

> *'At certain moments I see the pointlessness of it – work-ing like mad on a rowing machine to shave a tenth of a second off my time. But then I take a step back and see the privilege of being able to do this and what that tenth of a second might mean.'*

Throughout his career Adam has shown a relentless attention to detail. I asked him about this and why it was so important for him. His answer, although specific to his particular situation, is revealing:

> *'A third key filter is what I call the "actual behaviour" filter. An important technique we use at Channel 4 Online is one called "user-centred design". It requires you to focus on your end-users' or customers' needs and the*

detail of their circumstances and context. With that in mind, you have to ask: Is this really what people do? Will they really be bothered to do that? This is a real attention-to-detail thing. Where are they sitting relative to the screen? Who's in the room? How's the interaction controlled? Who's got the controlling device? And it's also those detailed little things that make the big difference. Look at the iPhone. Arguably not the greatest phone in the world but it's quite a pleasure to use. For example, it has little animations when you send a text that, although they are not strictly needed, turn it from being a functional experience into a pleasurable and satisfying one.'

Being 'me'

In Chapter 2 I emphasised how important it was that, whatever you do, you should be true to yourself, even if you accept that sometimes compromises have to be made. It's really hard to be happy if you can't express what it is that makes you 'you' in some way – to have an outlet for your individuality. A quote from Jonathan captures this well:

'In the kind of role I perform I have been able to take a step back and see what it takes for others to succeed. In recent years I have been worked with two of Britain's largest legal practices so my comments refer to lawyers, but I am sure they apply in many other working environments. First, it can be useful to be popular, but as one of my colleagues said once: "If you

*are successful, you will have your critics". Clearly you
also need to be an outstanding performer but a degree
of individuality – something that puts you in a different place – helps. For example, in law we have lots of
lawyers who can lock themselves in a room and pore
over a 150-page document for an hour or two and dis-
sect it well. That's important. But actually what is valued
above all else is the ability to win new business. And
that needs excellent interpersonal skills – being person-
able, confident and seeing things from the client's point
of view. Very bright people such as lawyers can easily
get lost in their own world.'*

The phrase 'We are all unique' has become one of life's
truisms – so heavily quoted that it has become trite. But
despite its ubiquity I absolutely believe it. That doesn't
mean that you and I have to love and cherish the unique
qualities of every person we come across – some of this
'uniqueness' might be irritating at best. The attempts by
some in the personality profiling industry to force us into a
few symbolically interesting but meaningless stereotypes as
though they were 'absolutes' have done us few favours here.

You are one of seven billion one-off stereotypes and are far
more interesting for being so. The world needs individuality
like never before. As Jonathan's quote says, there is a need
for 'something that puts you in a different place'. What is it
for you? What do you offer that others don't? How can you
retain and express your individuality?

What's the point? – summary

- Be clear about how what you do relates to what others do – you are not the end, you are the beginning. What do people want from you?

- Climb in to other people's worlds to understand their needs better.

- What role or roles do you perform best when you are part of a group?

- The detail separates the star performers from the 'just good enough' – there is a point to that little bit of extra effort.

- Be you.

LUCK FACTOR 11 – THINKING WITHOUT THINKING

'It's important to challenge assumptions about ways of doing things. Just because there is no precedent for doing something a particular way ... well, as often as not, that's probably a damned good reason to do it that new way!' ADAM

Generating ideas

There's never enough time. Deadlines loom, inboxes groan with unread email, to-do lists run over pages and pages and somewhere in all of this comes our 'spare time' for friends, families and hobbies. We put so much pressure on ourselves to be constantly doing that we miss all the possibilities we might have imagined if we had given ourselves the time to think properly.

This Luck Factor isn't about the minutiae of how to generate ideas or problem solve or spot opportunities. It's about how to create the conditions to allow you to do the things that are vital to our chances of being lucky. To do this you'll need to open up your mind and think in ways that you might not have considered. Here is a four-step process to help you do this.

Step 1 – Define and rephrase

It is easy to take a problem and, through the way you phrase the problem, create your own wall around it. Imagine that you get to work by car and the journey is always stressful. You don't much feel like doing any work when you arrive. You know you have a problem. So you define the problem thus: 'I need to get to work in a less stressed state *but* the traffic is always appalling.'

That word 'but' is a real idea killer and a statement like this, while strictly true, doesn't leave much scope for generating ideas. In fact there is a resigned 'What can I do?' acceptance about it. You need to rephrase the problem in such a way that makes it easier to generate solutions. For example, take these two statements:

- 'I need to arrive at work in a less stressed state *and* so I need to find ways of reducing that stress during my morning journey.'
- 'I need to arrive at work in a less stressed state *so* I should look at alternative ways of getting to work. What are the options?'

For the first statement you might come up with answers like: turn off the radio, play relaxing music, leave earlier and find a different, more scenic route. For the second statement you might look at travelling by train, cycling, car sharing, a combination of transport methods, finding a different, more scenic route and working from home more.

In our examples here we have shifted the statement from a problem to a question/statement of positive intent.

Step 2 – Reduce the pressure

In our busy state of constant doing we often set false deadlines, which are in the end only fools' deadlines and do nothing but add pressure. This doesn't allow the brain to work at its best. Crushing deadlines demand instant answers, and when forced to think the brain can only deliver ideas that are obvious, one-dimensional and a rehash of what has already been done.

Stop. Question the importance of the deadline and see if you can extend it – particularly where the deadline is self-imposed. Too often we assume that instant action is required, when it isn't, and often you can find a few more days (a couple of weeks would be even better). Greater insight comes to those who are able to give the brain time to work to its full capability.

Psychologist Guy Claxton has referred to this, combined with step 3 below, as 'the slow way of knowing'.

Step 3 – Apply the mental dimmer switch

So, you've reduced the pressure. Now give the brain time to work. Switch on the 'mental dimmer switch' and stop thinking about the problem or opportunity for a while. Take yourself away from it. A mental dimmer switch won't turn your brain off but it will shed a subtler, sexier light on whatever it is you are pondering. At a conscious level your brain produces ideas that are vanilla flavoured because these are the easiest to access, but remember that your brain also works on so many different levels.

The dimmer switch gives your brain a chance to think in different ways – dimming your conscious thinking helps you to think more deeply. Your brain is still working on things when you are consciously not. Think about when your best ideas come into your head – in the bath, driving or cycling, having a shower – but probably not when you are thinking 'hard' about problems. Soften up the whole process.

Step 4 – Capture and develop

How seriously do you take your ideas? If ideas do jump into your head at the unlikeliest moments, you need to capture your thoughts. Why?

- Because they may well be lost if you don't. The 3.00 a.m. eureka moment can become the 8.00 a.m. hazy recollection.
- Because most initial thoughts and ideas are not an end point. They are just a beginning. You and others will build on these thoughts, modify them and improve them until you can see a way to make them better.

A friend of mine once installed a whiteboard in his shower because that was where he had his best ideas and he was afraid of losing them if he didn't record them right then.

Thinking without thinking – summary

- Slow down – allow your thoughts to catch up with you.
- Turn down the pressure and give time for your best thoughts to hatch.
- Don't leave your thoughts lying around until they get forgotten.
- Rephrase and rethink your problems.
- Avoid saying 'Not invented here'.
- Enjoy what makes you different.

LUCK FACTOR 12 – KEEPING FRESH

'I know the catalysts for me. A couple of years ago I went to fashion designer Paul Smith's offices in Covent Garden, with some colleagues from Channel 4, and I was really struck by the stuff he had lying around. It reminded me that I have "stuff" dotted around my home, objects I like that spark my imagination. Props from shoots. Souvenirs from trips. Related to that, I find I use art quite a lot. An occasional sortie to the cinema or an art gallery, even in the middle of a working day – I need that inspiration to charge up the creative batteries again.' ADAM

OK, you might be thinking 'lucky you' for being able to pop into an art gallery during working hours, but the point here is clear. We need to know how, when or where we are able to regenerate ourselves – to have some sort of hinterland that provides a step back from the harsher world of top performance for a recharge. Most people seem to need this although some do love what they do so much that the idea of 'escape', no matter how brief, does not register as a need.

Here is a health warning. Achievement for its own sake is not so good. There has to be meaning attached to those achievements otherwise you can end up feeling 'flat' – the existential 'What am I actually here for?' question rears up. This can happen at the most unexpected times. Take 2008 Olympic cycling gold-medallist Victoria Pendleton who talked about her own flat feeling after winning gold and finding it difficult to create 'meaning' for herself when competing afterwards. You can lose the meaning even for things you love doing (and Pendleton has often said that she really enjoys training). That's when you know you need a break.

First-time experiences

In Chapter 1, in the Luck Habit questionnaire, I asked you to think when was the last time you did something for the first time. How long did you have to think about it? If you skipped the questionnaire, consider the question now. It's a good starting point because it challenges you to think about the new stimuli you have had in your life over the last year or so.

If you get totally wrapped up in what you are doing you will eventually stop performing at your best because you have been starved of the stimuli that come from new and temporarily diverting activities or thinking.

Everyday living can desensitise us – almost as though we were in a zombie-like state. You deprioritise or forget your pleasurable leisure activities. You may be the sort of person who loves the cinema or going to a football match, but what with everything else you find you can go a whole year without doing either of these things. Or, like the majority of the population, you may find yourself eating the same five meals for dinner every day of every week. Time for a rethink.

A good way to appreciate new things – and to reintroduce yourself to old stimuli – is to give your five senses a workout. Here is a useful exercise to help you think about the last time you consciously stimulated each of your senses, combined with a list of the possibilities for doing so in the near future.

FIVE SENSES

Sense	The last time?	The next time?
Taste	----------------------	----------------------
Touch	----------------------	----------------------
Sight	----------------------	----------------------
Smell	----------------------	----------------------
Hearing	----------------------	----------------------

Suggestions for 'the next time' might include (please forgive a few personal ones here):

- **Taste**. Good wine, really flavoursome food (cooked by yourself, so accessing 'touch' too).

- **Touch**. Soil, skin (with silk!), food, wood, plants, your partner, water, animal fur.

- **Sight**. The highest point in your town, a new place each week no matter how local, art, a football match, the night sky.

- **Smell**. The countryside, a forest after rain, fresh coffee, the sea.

- **Hearing**. Music (live or recorded), real silence, ambient sounds, sports crowds, libraries, the dawn chorus.

A few ideas

Here are a few ideas for getting the freshness back:

- **A holiday at home**. This is something that a lot of people don't consider. I realised the power of it in my own life a few years ago when, living in London, I decided to have a holiday in London rather than go elsewhere. As a tourist in your own neighbourhood you see things that you normally take for granted. But this does something else that's really important. If you tell yourself 'Home – bad, away – good' the grey cloud over current surroundings is tough to shift when, in actuality, your locale could be so much more interesting than the place you are planning to go to. This is not an argument for not going anywhere. Far from it. But it is an argument for feeling positive about your local surroundings and to remind yourself to appreciate what is in front of you from time to time.

- **Knowing your catalysts**. Remind yourself about what regenerates you – we all have touchstones that help us. Cinema, sport, silence, comedy or a good meal? Getting bogged down can mean forgetting or even losing your touchstones. Domestic circumstances can flip you into 'What I can't do' mode rather than the more positive 'What I can do' that sparks energising thoughts.

- **Curiosity**. Journeys into the unknown are healthy too. If you seek out only those things that already interest you you may never find anything new to be interested in. This is limiting, though increasingly likely as you get older. As Trinidadian Marxist, writer and lover of cricket C.L.R. James once said: 'What do they know of cricket whom only cricket know?' You need to do some psychological travelling – taking your mind to new places. Write down a list of 20 or 30 things you could do – for example, you could read about something you know nothing about, put something random into Google and see where it takes you, have a go at a sport you've never tried before, write a short story, sing or try a tough mental challenge. Do not judge your list – think freely. Now ask 'How could I do some of those things?'

Keeping fresh – summary

- Appreciate what's around you, accessible and even free.

- Stimulate all your senses regularly.

- Entertain regular first-time experiences.

- Know your catalysts – the things you can easily access that relax you and give you pleasure.

- Try to do one thing for yourself each day – even just for a few moments.

CHAPTER 5

Purpose

'I always have a better sense of what I don't want to do than what I do want to do. I work on an 18-month horizon. If my next 18 months look interesting then I don't have itchy feet. I don't have this massive vision or this massive career plan like some do. My life plan is to be always interested in what I am doing.' ADAM

Luck Factors in this chapter:

Luck Factor 13 – Having life-defining goals

Luck Factor 14 – Having a horizon

Luck Factor 15 – Living in the moment

The purpose of this chapter is to look at goals. There is no accepted wisdom about this. Some of us like to have clear, tightly defined goals that take us step-by-step through life, and which build up into a clearly-thought-through womb-to-tomb success strategy. Some of us, like Adam in his quote, like to have direction – to feel that what is ahead of them is stimulating and motivating – but they do not define their goals tightly. Others are very happy to live in the moment.

You might be asking, 'Which is best?' The answer is that they are all great, so you need to choose which is right for you and the kind of person you are. You can't be forced into the life goal for which you feel little or no affinity or for which the timescale renders it meaningless for you. And neither can you live an ad hoc life if your preference is for clear purpose. My feeling is that the vast majority of us do need purpose in our lives and this chapter concerns itself with two aspects of this:

- Having life-defining goals.
- Having a horizon.

To balance this I strongly believe that life becomes very dull if we see it as a succession of tightly defined short-term and long-term goals. So, in a third section, we'll look at living in the moment. You probably have an orientation to only one of these three attitudes and that is fine, so in this sense these three Luck Factors are not like the other 17. However, my sense is that all three lock together and we need some of all of them. As one of our interviewees, Michele, says:

> 'I have had my "life plan". I wanted to go to China when I was younger and I did. I worked there for two years. I tend to live more in the moment now. I've no idea what I will be doing in five years' time but I know what I'd like to be doing in general terms. I'm certainly reinvigorated by new challenges.'

The spontaneity from being prepared to 'live in the moment', for some of the time at least, is healthy. This spontaneity develops an interest … the interest becomes more than just a passing phase … the passing phase becomes something lifelong … the life-defining goals (Luck Factor 13) kick in. We start to want to be better at whatever it is that has captured us, or to develop the interest and create a structure round it that helps us take it a little further.

In the field of achievement – whether in career, sporting pursuits or hobbies – I often hear the words 'You're so lucky to be doing what you're doing'. Show me the person about whom this is said and I can show you, in most cases, the person who has worked very hard, who identified early opportunities or used their imagination to create something for themselves and then pursued it. Old-school 'luck' has little to do with it. The Luck Habit does.

LUCK FACTOR 13 – HAVING LIFE-DEFINING GOALS

For many people having a 'life goal' – often hatched when quite young – never really moves from fantasy to reality. Circumstances take over, which are often used as an excuse for not putting in the sheer hard work required for dream-fulfilment. The dream is lovely. The idea of the hard work, less so. Your willingness to put in this effort is determined by how much you really want to do the thing you dream about. The person who compromises on the hard work or manages to find better things to do probably didn't want to do it enough.

To succeed you need a clear balance between the heart (which provides emotional drive) and the head (which provides the clear-sighted, logical thinking that turns the life goal – the dream, the fantasy – into a plan of action). There will be setbacks along the way, which will also test your 'desire'. This Luck Factor looks at the emotional side of having a life goal – the heart. The mechanics of how this might be achieved, for instance setting milestones along the way, are looked at in the following Luck Factor 'Having a horizon'. In this first Luck Factor I use the experiences of Boeing 747 pilot Bernice Moran as a base point and then address each of the issues raised in more detail.

Case study – Bernice Moran on flying

In the introduction I profiled Bernice Moran. She became Europe's youngest female captain for a commercial airline (Ryanair) when she was 27 and has since gone on to be a pilot flying 747s for Virgin Atlantic. She provides an instructive case study in what it takes to get there because she hatched this desire from the age of six or seven. When Bernice was nine her mother died and the money that might have been available to nurture Bernice's desire to fly had to be curtailed as her father focused his efforts on raising his three children. But at the age of ten she got herself into the cockpit of the plane, was allowed very briefly to take the controls and got, as she says, 'the fire in my belly'. (See below: '1 Testing desire'.)

With the fire still there Bernice went through school and on to University College Dublin. She had lots of fun at university but she didn't just idle away her time in the student bar. She got a job selling underwear in a Dublin department store so that she could fund flying lessons. She graduated and on the day of her graduation her father, seeing how serious and determined she was, agreed to help with finance. (See below: '2 Hard work and attraction'.)

Bernice got her pilot's licence and then trained with, and flew for Ryanair, flying Boeing 737s. There have been setbacks but, as she says herself, losing your mother at the age of nine makes almost anything that follows relatively unimportant. She has developed a thick skin:

> *'One of the challenges I get is being a woman flying a plane. Only 1 per cent of airline pilots are women. If I pop out from the flight deck I often get handed coats and things or asked for a Coke because some passengers assume that women are always stewardesses. I have to be humble here, I can't be a "madam" about this. So I hang their coats up. Or I get a Coke. That's on the lighter side. On the more serious side there are still plenty of people who don't think a woman should be anywhere near the controls of a passenger plane. As a result, where anyone else can get away with being average, I have to be better than that.'*

(See below: '3 Toughening up'.)

> *'Even when I was a captain at Ryanair I had a deep desire to work for Virgin Atlantic – they are a bit quirky and fun and I really identified with that. I thought they would be perfect for me. I banged on their door many times and*

suffered the pain of rejection once when I thought I was in, but I persisted and eventually they took me. I was at last flying 747s for a company I really wanted to work for. A long-term goal had been achieved.'

(See below: '4 One goal leads to another'.)

So, let's draw some key points from this:

1 Testing desire

A good first lesson, with any big personal goals, is to test how much you really like something by having a go at it. If the fire is really ignited then you know you have the necessary emotional propulsion to get through the hard work and the setbacks. Just as you will be tested all along the way (as we have seen with Bernice), you need to test yourself early on.

What sounds good in theory may be different in practice, and this allows you to relate the dream to the reality. It's why, for example, if a 15-year-old wants to be a vet it would be a very good idea for them to help out in the local vet's surgery during a school holiday. It's why, too, the great January new year's resolution becomes forgotten a month later as the expensive gym membership doesn't get used (my local swimming pool – packed at lunchtime in January – is half empty four weeks later). What sounded good in principle was not the same in practice. This all leads back to the affinity we looked at in Luck Factor 1.

2 Hard work and attraction

If people see you are serious about something they start to take you seriously. You find yourself attracting people who might be able to help you. So, if people aren't noticing your desire, are you demonstrating how serious you are about it? This seriousness is expressed in commitment and hard work, and often involves sacrifice. If you enjoy the autobiographies of the successful you'll know that in many cases that success came with sacrifices along the way. There are few short cuts. This is where your desire really gets tested.

3 Toughening up

Here is an important lesson about perspective. Bernice is able to compare any challenges and setbacks against one of the worst things we could imagine happening to someone so young. A lot of the small challenges (such as other people assuming she can't be a pilot because she is a woman) she laughs at.

So, how do you toughen up, particularly if you are highly sensitive and don't have Bernice's comparative experience? First, a degree of sensitivity is a good thing. Without it you won't recognise the problems and opportunities around your goals, and neither will you have much empathy for others, which is an essential skill for success. But too much sensitivity and you will talk yourself out of action.

Here are some suggestions to help you toughen up:

- **Remember you are not the centre of the world**. Other people have their own worlds. Don't project everything back to yourself. Instead ask: 'While this is a priority for me, I understand it may not be for someone else. So how can I make people interested in my needs without alienating them?' Work on the basis that the more interested you are in the needs of others, the more interested they are likely to be in yours.

- **Practise patience and self-control**. Things do take time. Emotional, impulsive behaviour comes before rational thinking and is often triggered by the amygdala in the brain. It is very good when we need a 'fight or flight' response (because you don't have time to think) but not so useful where considered rather than emotional reactions are needed. Some of us learn to override these emotional reactions through experience. Some don't. It's easy to create a mini-crisis and an instant response when things haven't quite worked out. Often a little considered thinking will be far more useful and get better results. This needs patience.

- **Don't over-analyse**. Analysis is good. Too much and you stop. Focus back on your goals. Are the questions and analysis really helping you to focus on your specific goals? Are they relevant?

- **Use the protecting shell statement**. This helps when things don't go the way you planned them. The protecting shell statement helps to shelter you and me from disproportionate emotional damage when things don't work out. Two examples:

- 'OK, this is normal. I can't expect everything to go smoothly. What's important is that I take a deep breath, take time to look at what went wrong and come up with new ideas.'

- 'It's a setback but I won't let this get to me. I need to think about what went wrong and do my best to make sure it won't happen again. I've got to keep a sense of perspective about this. Other people have much bigger problems to deal with. I will get through this.'

4 One goal leads to another

Although a degree of single mindedness is good, our eyes need to be open and our gaze wide enough to see that other paths are available. In Bernice's case this meant that once the goal of pilot had been achieved, new goals (captain for Ryanair, flying 747s for Virgin Atlantic) opened up. In the last chapter ('Opportunity') I take this logic further as one opportunity taken opens lots of others – once you take the lid off the tin it's hard to get it back on again.

How might someone else tackle a big goal?

I am always surprised by the way we put walls around our own ambitions ('I can't do this now because …') and yet apply very different thinking to the lives of friends and colleagues ('Go for it', 'You can do it'). If you use Facebook you have probably seen how encouraging friends are with each other (although that encouragement can at times seem to have an air of superficiality about it). With friends we see the reasons to do things before we search for the reasons not to. The attainment of the big life goals and life changes don't succeed without planning and careful thought. But the positive 'I can do this' perspective comes first.

Defining a goal – the Hollywood summary

You may have heard of the 25-word film-idea summary that Hollywood bosses ask scriptwriters and producers to give them. They often make their commissioning decisions based on these summaries. A great example is *Alien*, which was pitched as 'Jaws in space'.

Applying this practice to your own goal setting (big or small goals) is a nice way to have a clearly defined goal to work towards. This absolute clarity is so important – vagueness about the goal will mean vagueness about the achieving of it. Timing is also important. Here are some examples:

- By January 2020 I will be certified to fly Boeing 737 aeroplanes on commercial flights.
- By July 2018 I will have passed A level/Baccalaureate Spanish and be able to converse freely in that language.
- By July 2018 I will have my Certificate in Education so that I can be a full-time teacher.

The timing of goal achievement will need to be realistic. This Hollywood summary then gives you something to work back from as you define the stepping-stones that will get you to achieve the goal. These stepping-stones will also test the viability of your big goal – you can always change the timings. In Luck Factor 14 we look at how to create these stepping-stones, with a couple of worked examples.

Having life-defining goals – summary

- Have a clearly defined goal with (if appropriate) timings.

- Be sure that the goal is motivating.

- Your seriousness about achieving your goal will mean potential helpers will take you seriously.

- You won't achieve your goal without very hard work.

- Have some strategies for dealing with setbacks.

LUCK FACTOR 14 – HAVING A HORIZON

The difference between 'having a horizon' and a 'life-defining goal' is that you can see the horizon, whereas the life-defining goal is likely to be so big that it is not 'see-able'. To achieve the life-defining goal you need to divide it into chunks – what I call here specific horizons. If you are one of those people who doesn't want or have a life-defining goal you can use these horizons to set the shorter goals that work better for you.

Some shorter-term goals can be used to identify and maximise an opportunity. For example, perhaps you want to go back to studying so that you can become a teacher. So you define the goal, to use an example from the previous Luck Factor, as: 'By July 2018 I will have my Certificate in Education so that I can be a full-time teacher'. You then resolve to take the steps to achieve this.

The goal you have may be set in response to a problem. Deciding to qualify to be a teacher might be a reaction to unhappiness in a current job or a mismatch between the person and the job. In this way the negative of unhappiness or mismatch is turned into a positive action goal statement, which is much more motivating for you. You must feel an affinity for the goal statement you select – in this example deciding to go into teaching. The affinity provides the essential emotional propulsion for you to go for it.

There is also a sensory aspect to these horizons, well expressed by Adam in his introductory quote:

> '*I always have a better sense of what I don't want to do than what I do want to do. I work on an 18-month horizon. If my next 18 months look interesting then I don't have itchy feet.*'

I took the 'horizon' element of this Luck Factor from his quote. I do not want to give the impression that goal setting has always has a rigidity about it. For Adam, it means an 18-month timeline in which things look interesting for him. If it doesn't, he does something about it. For Michele (as shown in her earlier quote), living in the moment is important, but she is also able to see the need for change too:

> '*I've no idea what I will be doing in five years' time but I know what I'd like to be doing in general terms. I'm certainly reinvigorated by new challenges.*'

The perfect goal?

> '*In the past, I might have said something because I was seeking some sort of perfection. Part of my wisdom now is to realise that there is not always a perfect blueprint. It's better to go with what everyone believes is the right thing to do.*' GREG

I have chosen to use Greg's quote here because it does two things in relation to goal setting. First, because it touches on the frustration you may feel if you have tried to define specific goals for yourself, or where these may have been imposed on you if you operate in a more formal work environment (appraisal interviews are often the means by which this is done). Second, because his quote reinforces the point about the need to feel affinity for what you individually – or in his case collectively – are trying to achieve.

Experts talk about the need to be specific in your goal setting. If sport is your thing then the end goal of winning or achieving a particular time or finishing in a particular place in a league table makes the job of specificity easier. However, what Greg's quote suggests to me is that, even in the world of sport, where there is a defined end game, the means by which you get there are varied. This leads us neatly into our specific 'horizons' where, after setting a motivating end goal for yourself, we meet the challenge of how you get there.

The specific horizon

'I knew that I needed a boost. I saw an ad in Melody Maker *magazine looking for someone to jam with, so I replied and met Tim Crowther, who gave me a very clear sense of what I had to do. He said I was a good player but I needed to learn the basic tools of improvisation, such as modes, scales, and most importantly how chords "worked". I made a decision. I was going to give myself a year to get to the level I needed to be at to make music a full-time career. At that time I was working in a day job that was slowly eating away at my soul, so I was very motivated to make the change.*

I developed a strict practice plan and stuck to it dog-gedly and at the end of the year I handed in my notice and became a full-time guitar player. I picked up studio work along the way and was able to regularly play live in different bands.' MO

Mo expresses the need he had for a strict practice plan to get him to the level of musicianship he wanted to be at. The first step here is to undertake a mental rehearsal. To ask, 'If I was going to do this, what might the steps be?' Having defined those steps (and asking experts will help) you then order them. In this Luck Factor there are two examples of how this could be done.

Example 1 Learning a language

As our first example we will look at learning a language. In this case the language is Spanish. First there has to be a purpose, no matter how vague. The purpose has to be energising for you. It could be:

■ I need Spanish for my work.

■ I want mental stimulation.

■ I am interested in learning more about the culture.

■ I am ashamed that I don't know a foreign language at all and this seems a good one to start with.

■ Some of my family come from Spain and I want to talk to them.

■ I want to get a qualification.

Or a combination of the above. The goal has also been defined – with a deadline:

'By July 2018 I will have passed A level/Baccalaureate in Spanish and be able to converse freely in that language.'

So, now we put together a series of timelines to get you to the point where the goal has been reached. It could go like this:

- Year One (2013–14):

  Action – To enrol in evening classes at my local college.

  Achievement – To have mastered basic sentences such as 'What is your name?'. To learn 500 words of vocabulary (10 per week). To know the present tense of key verbs.

- Year Two (2014–15):

  Action – To continue with evening classes. To visit Spain for two weeks and make a conscious effort to speak only Spanish with Spanish people.

  Achievement – To learn a further 500 words of vocabulary. To work through future and past tenses of key verbs.

- Year Three (2015–16):

  Action – To continue evening classes combined with a monthly visit to a private tutor where I practise my spoken Spanish. To make two visits to Spain.

  Achievement – To read a Spanish book, even if I don't understand all of it (have a dictionary beside me). To take my first GCSE/national equivalent Spanish exam and pass at the top grade.

- Year Four (2016–17):

  Action – To have fortnightly sessions with my private tutor. To study for ten hours per week. To make two visits to Spain.

Achievement – To pass the advance level mock exam beyond minimum grade.

- Year Five (2017–18)

Action – As per year four.

Achievement – To pass the advance level exam with an A or B grade (or equivalent).

This sets out a useful series of timelines with actions and intended achievements. This should not be rigid. I cannot vouch for the specific accuracy of the timelines in reality and, where it is a learning goal, expert input from a tutor or class teacher should be sought. The timelines as well as the final goal need to be realistic.

Example 2 Giving a presentation

The language example was a big goal that was broken up into smaller parts that are instantly see-able. In the next example I am going to continue with a theme running through this book – giving a presentation. This is a short-term goal, where a critical presentation is going to be delivered in one month's time by a speaker who is not confident.

Day 1	Decide on the presentation's key objective and 'ponder' for a few days (see Luck Factor 11).
Day 7	Brainstorm potential subject matter for the presentation (possibly with others).
Day 10	Create a structure (around three key points that support the objective).

	Edit subject matter – decide what's in and what isn't.
Day 15	Write the presentation.
Day 20	Prepare visuals if needed (PowerPoint, Prezi, Keynote) and other visual and audio props that may be required.
Day 25	Dry run with a small group.
	Anticipate likely questions (with group).
Day 26	Make adjustments based on the group's feedback.
Day 29	A further practice.
Day 30	Give presentation.
Afterwards	Get feedback and make a note of what went well and what can be improved for next time.

This 'afterwards' is what can get missed out. How did it go? Is there any feedback from the audience? In achieving goals the review is an important part of your own learning.

Having stimulating horizons

Here are some tips to help you generate horizons that work for you:

- Know yourself – understand what it is that stimulates you.
- Make sure you have projects ahead of you that provide that stimulation.
- Be an initiator – use your creative capacity to generate ideas and opportunities that will create the stimulating projects for you.

- Develop stronger relationships through networking etc. with people who are stimulated in similar ways and share your values, interests and motivations.

- Have multiple horizons. Working on one doesn't mean that others shouldn't be up and running too.

As much as anything these horizons are about spotting and taking opportunities. This is dealt with in more detail in Chapter 7.

Having a horizon – summary

- Have a specific problem-solving or opportunity-taking goal.

- You must, *must* feel motivated to achieve it – this will be clarified by the purpose of the goal.

- Identify timelines so that you can monitor your progress.

- Be clear on the risk factors.

- Use your senses to feel what is interesting and motivating for you in the near future.

- Try not to limit yourself to one goal.

LUCK FACTOR 15 – LIVING IN THE MOMENT

'Having [a goal] is generally deemed a good thing. The benefit of something to strive toward. This can also blind you, however: you see only your goal, and nothing else, while this something else – wider, deeper – may be considerably more interesting and important.'
RYSZARD KAPUŚCIŃSKI, *The Shadow of the Sun*

You've probably come across the phrase 'goal-blindness'. A situation where you become so fixated by a specific goal that you fail to appreciate what is around you now. This fixation is also damaging in cases where progress renders your specific goal obsolete and meaningless because of what is going on in the outside world. This applies particularly where modern technologies are concerned.

But there is a third and compelling reason for you not to become fixated. I mentioned earlier that Olympic gold-medal-winning cyclist Victoria Pendleton confessed to feeling rather flat after her achievement. Greg Searle said that he didn't really know how to celebrate at the moment he won his gold medal. There can be a 'What now?' feeling. Some psychologists talk of the importance of the journey in relation to reaching the end destination. Sigmund Freud related that, with hindsight, the struggle is often more enjoyable than the achievement. Both Victoria Pendleton and Greg Searle are very clear that they enjoy the 'struggle'.

Life is not just one tightly prescribed chase to achieve rigid goals. In fact the relaxed frame of mind that comes from enjoying simple pleasures in life can help you achieve your bigger goals. Of course that shouldn't compromise the discipline needed to achieve them. Sitting in the pub every night is not a good way to help your studies. Once a week, however, can be very healthy. I don't have a deep analytical well on which to draw this final point other than that which I have observed, but it seems to me that those whose sole focus is the final achievement tend not enjoy it as much if they haven't also enjoyed the steps that led up to it.

The message here is to relish, not ignore, captured moments of spontaneity. And while these 'captured moments of spontaneity' are great, there are also specific things you can do that get you out of run-of-the-mill routines and put you in a position where unexpected – but enjoyable – things are more likely to happen. So, whether you live your whole life 'in the moment' or need a counterweight to the defined goals you are pursuing, here are a few ideas for enjoying the moment:

Specific acts

Here you determine to do a different activity on a regular basis. In the Luck Habit questionnaire in Chapter 1 I suggested going to the highest point in your town or village as indicative of a curiosity about local surroundings. One elderly man I knew created his own version of this and determined that every single day he would go to a place in his town he had never been to before – even if it was a shop or a side street that superficially didn't look interesting. He reported that he never struggled to find new things in his locality.

Simple pleasures

Positive-psychology guru Martin Seligman has a simple technique he uses when he goes to bed that allows him to think about what's been good about his day, rather than the negative stuff. He simply thinks back to three things he has enjoyed during the day – simple pleasures – and remembers them for a moment. These really can be simple things. Having a coffee with an old friend you haven't seen for a while; a great piece of music; something that made you laugh; a half-hour activity with your children; a walk. It's just a reminder that some of the most enjoyable things in life are unrehearsed.

Listen to your heart

Some people find it easier to recall feelings than specific events. In spontaneous activity it's our heart telling us to go on and enjoy ourselves. The heart tells the head what to do. It's not a template for life, but it is a healthy guide for letting a bit of spontaneity in. You must be able to do this from time to time without feeling guilty. Otherwise you do not enjoy the moment like you should because you are worrying about what else you should be doing.

Pay attention to the present

It's easy to slip into comparative mode – thinking about somewhere else we want to be, for example on holiday, or how this particular meal isn't as good as the last one we had here. Enjoy *now*. Try not to rush the things you enjoy – such as a good meal (avoid the ghastly habit of eating at the desk) or a good book (try not to speed read a book you really like).

Don't get down about what you really cannot do

Writers on positive thinking in the past have encouraged you to work on your weaknesses and suggested that, if you work hard enough, you can turn them into strengths. I would say yes, but only if you have an affinity with the activity concerned and you sense progress – although there will be things we have to master, at work for example, whether we enjoy them or not.

There are things you enjoy doing, even if you are currently not so good at them. You don't have a fixed level of capability at anything and it is the engagement that you get through enjoyment that will be the primary mastery driver. But there are probably some things that are just plainly demoralising for you – you don't enjoy them and you never will. For me it's anything to do with fixing cars and anything to do with DIY. You shouldn't always strive to be better at something you get no joy from when there is a chance to go off and do something more personally enriching.

The ambiguity of experimentation

Some people don't like ambiguity. And some people like the unknown. Bernice, one of the interviewees, says: 'I try new things out of devilness – I enjoy the uncertainty' ... but not, let me assure you, when she is flying a 747.

Some of us can relate to this uncertainty. 'Playing' around with something new has the twin benefit of temporary respite from the day-to-day stuff and the possibility that it could open up a new and interesting path for you. Getting good at something combines the ambiguity of experimentation with at certain points the need to 'get your head down' and define a clear plan for improvement. So, living in the moment has a very discernable connection with setting goals.

Doing nothing

Oh, and finally, since much of this book is about success and achievement and positivity and performance, it is actually a very good thing once in a while to sit in a chair for an hour and do absolutely nothing – TV off, no laptop/ internet, soft light and relaxed breathing.

Living in the moment – summary

- Relish the benefits of temporary purposelessness.

- Welcome spontaneity.

- Enjoy instant, simple pleasures.

- It's OK to let your pleasure-seeking heart rule your sensible head once in a while.

CHAPTER 6

People

'A really important thing for me – and this applies to anyone involved in communication in any discipline – is the ability to see and feel from other people's perspectives. I am often surprised by how poorly developed many people's skills are in this area. It is critical for me as developer of multi-platform programmes (TV programmes integrated with the web, mobile phones/ devices and real-life activity) and as a scriptwriter, and it is just as critical if you are, say, a marketer or even a writer of instruction manuals. You have to be able to take a step back and take a view on what this feels like from the target audience's, the user's, the consumer's point of view. I see bad examples of this all the time. A really common example is the way people fail so often to spot jargon in what they write or present. It is a clear sign to an audience of someone who doesn't understand their perspective, or doesn't care.' ADAM

Luck Factors in this chapter:

Luck Factor 16 – Behaviour breeds behaviour

Luck Factor 17 – Networking

Luck Factor 18 – Influencing

Luck Factor 19 – Sharing success

This is a chapter about other people and how you relate to them. It is not a chapter about manipulation, deception or forcing people to do what you want them to. Neither is a chapter about being everybody's friend. It is about seeing people as an important part of your life because, if you want to get results, to perform at your best and to achieve your goals, you will not do these things alone – they happen through people, not despite them.

For some of us this means readjusting our view of people – from the 'barrier' to the ally. Most of us, of course, don't see people generally as barriers (notwithstanding the odd problem person) but we still need to be more proactive in the way we develop relationships. It's no secret that this investment in people rewards you personally and professionally.

We'll start by looking at the skills that help you make the best connections – how you listen and question, and how interested you are in the worlds of others. We'll also look at how to operate with people you don't feel an affinity for. It's my subjective view that it's the way you relate to this group of people that can make the difference between success and failure.

Then I'll give you the techniques you need to master two very contemporary people skills – networking and influencing – before the chapter finishes by looking at how you share the good times – praise, words of appreciation for the help and support you were given, and how you see success.

We start with the best of intentions – hell is not, as was claimed by Jean-Paul Sartre, 'other people'.

LUCK FACTOR 16 – BEHAVIOUR BREEDS BEHAVIOUR

There are seven billion people living on planet Earth. Each one is unique and has their own world view. If we are to strengthen our relationships with the people around us, we need to be curious and interested in how the world looks to them. Why? Because as human beings we are programmed emotionally and neurologically to be attracted to someone who is interested in us, listens to what we have to say, and has an appreciation of how we think, what we believe and what we need.

Developing the skills to really understand people will enable you to develop productive and happy relationships with the people in your world. After all, none of us operates in a vacuum and it's mainly through other people that we can achieve our ambitions.

Really knowing people well also helps you to manage your own expectations of them (although people can be gloriously unpredictable).

Travelling to other worlds

Being actively interested in the needs, thoughts, feelings and beliefs of other people is a life skill. It underpins those key strands of personal effectiveness such as assertiveness, influencing, negotiation and networking.

When you actively show an interest in other people, not only will they be drawn to you, but they will also respond to you on a deeper level because they realise that not only are you interested in them, but you also understand their needs and interests. This comes to the fore, for example, in negotiation situations where there are conflicting sets of interests: if you understand the person you are negotiating with and the needs that are driving their behaviour, you are in a far better position to find a resolution.

On a cruder level we all have a little strand in our thinking that asks 'What's in it for me?'. If you understand this and seek to establish this in those you interact with, you can influence better (the other person is thinking: 'OK, you want me to do this, what's in it for me?'); negotiate better (you say 'You've said this is particularly important to you, how about we agree …'); and network better because you understand the needs of your contacts.

Implicit within this 'travel to other worlds' is a core skill without which it is impossible to develop meaningful, productive relationships with people – knowing how to listen at a more committed level than people normally do.

Committed listening

Think closely about what stops you listening properly. You might come up with a list like this:

- The other person is boring.
- I got lost in my own thoughts.
- I'm tired.
- I have other priorities.
- I feel stressed.
- I've got something even more interesting to say.
- I strongly disagree with what the other person says.

In all cases there is one effect of all these and that is that you withdraw from the conversation. You are still physically present of course but your mind may be:

- Formulating a response – in which case you've stopped listening because you can't be listening properly and planning your response at the same time.
- Thinking about something entirely different (what you're going to do tonight, etc.).

You may have been surprised that the following were included on the list of listening barriers:

- I've got something even more interesting to say.
- I strongly disagree with what the other person says.

The reason I've placed them here is because, in the case of the first barrier, you say your more 'interesting' idea, or prepare to say it, and of course stop listening. In the case of the second, you either prepare your counter-argument or voice your disagreement, in which case you also stop listening.

I want to look at 'I got lost in my own thoughts' because this is where we tend to end up when we are not listening. The 'boring' other person or tiredness or stress or other priorities can all lead directly to this. Here we need what I call *committed* listening (you may have come across the similar 'active' or 'creative' listening). It can be very tough to listen to people you don't really connect with or with whom you disagree. But often you have to, even if you really want to be somewhere else.

The greater the level and depth of conversation in your own mind, the less you are able to listen properly to what's being said. So, the skill here is to keep these inner conversation diversions under wraps and refocus back on what is being said:

- Avoid the trap of improving the other person's story with one of your own.

- If your head says 'disagree', say something like: 'That's an interesting perspective, why do you see it that way?' or 'I hadn't thought of it that way ...'. Of course, in extreme situations, where someone says something morally or ethically repugnant, you may just want to walk off. (And do the same with verbal aggression.)

- Confirm back what you think you have heard. First, this is a good way of checking understanding, but it also keeps you mind focused on what's being said, rather than your own potentially diverting thoughts: 'I just want to be sure I have understood what you said. Are you saying …?'.

- Nod your head and add a few words to encourage the other person to continue (and to tell them you are actually listening): 'How did that make you feel?' or 'What were you thinking when it happened?' or 'Carry on, this is really interesting'.

- Engage your body in the conversation. The effects of your positive, open body language on the other person are well acknowledged. What's mentioned less are the subtle effects your body language has on you.

- Allow small gaps in conversation. While culturally in western countries we are less comfortable than, say, the Japanese with silence in conversation, nevertheless, a few seconds to ponder what has been said (and even to say 'I'm just thinking about what you've said') not only aids your own thinking process but sends out a strong signal that you are listening.

- If you get talking with someone who is boring or just goes on and on, and you need to cut in while they are speaking try using flattery to do it: 'Sorry to butt in, you made a really interesting point a moment ago and I just want to pick up on it …'. Or try paraphrasing: 'If I can just summarise, so what you are saying is …'.

If you look back over this section on committed listening you will see that good questioning also offers a framework to help you keep a conversation moving so that you can engage with someone. Good questioning leads to accurate thinking on your part – assuming that you are listening properly to what is said. Some of us have a curiosity that propels us to ask questions naturally. Most of us have to push ourselves a little to ask the extra question that may reveal a perspective, an anecdote, an observation or a contrary view that we would not have established if we didn't ask. This is about your willingness to establish what people think, need, feel and believe. Engage with genuine curiosity about other people's worlds and they will be more likely to engage with yours.

Expectations

Michele makes a lovely point about how she sees others when she wears her managerial hat: 'I am asking for your 100 per cent. And I am not looking for your 100 per cent to be the same as everybody else's.' This statement shows that she implicitly understands that everyone is different and we have to adjust our expectations of others based on our understanding of them.

Your expectations will not just be practical and skills-based. When you know someone well you are able to understand how they react in different situations. This means you can adjust your behaviour to the person and their reaction, rather than adopting a 'one-size-fits-all' approach to everyone.

Say you want to give a bit of feedback to a fellow member of your team. If you know that this person finds it hard to take feedback (perhaps they lack confidence or mistake feedback for damning criticism) and that they are likely to react emotionally, you can adjust your approach by wrapping up the feedback with praise for the things that they have done well. This means that not only do you avoid an upset team member, but you also enable them to get the benefit of the feedback as well as a boost to their confidence.

Greg was honest enough to admit to me that the issue of seeing things from another person's point of view was something that he thought about when looking back on his 2000 Olympics experience:

> *'With experience I have been able to reflect on the way I worked with others. I have learnt not to throw away the team dynamic. My partner in the boat at the 2000 Olympics, Ed Coode, was much less experienced than me and I could have thought about that more. I challenged him when things weren't going very well and I probably undermined his confidence.'*

80:15:5

In life roughly 80 per cent of the people you know will offer you satisfying and productive relationships. Another 5 per cent will be the opposite, and no matter what you do you will never have a happy time with them. It's easy to get hung up on these people but in all honesty it's easier and a more fruitful use of your time simply to cut them adrift.

The last group are the ones I'll focus on here – the 15 per cent. These people may be a bit of a struggle for various reasons but they are worth your investment of time and effort in improving the relationship because it will bring benefits to both of you.

So, you might be asking: 'How do I distinguish between one of the 5 per cent and one of the 15 per cent?' The answer is that initially you probably can't. What a lot of people do is to dump those with whom they have to work a bit harder into a group labelled 'difficult people' and then abandon them. Only when you have made a genuine effort to connect with the 20 per cent can you then break up the group further into 'tough but it can work' (the 15 per cent) and 'I've done my best, but it's just not happening' (the 5 per cent).

This 15 per cent are often the people who can make a real difference and while we may not feel any real affinity with them, if we are prepared to make the effort then the rewards are substantial. That old principle of 'behaviour breeding behaviour' comes in here.

Working with the more difficult in the 15 per cent group

The 15 per cent may be made of the following kinds of people:

- People with whom you feel you lack credibility.
- People who seem to disagree with you on a regular basis.
- People whose behaviour with you lacks consistency.
- People who see you as a 'threat'.
- People with aggressive behaviour, for example, who raise their voice.
- People who are unhelpful when you need something from them.

Here is a seven-step process about working with some of the more challenging 15 per cent to generate mutually beneficial outcomes. The flow diagram guides you from the start point – the problem – through to action. Each step is summarised below.

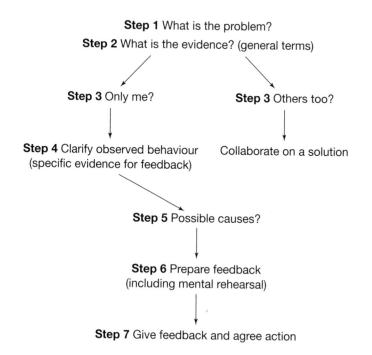

Step 1 What is the problem?
Step 2 What is the evidence? (general terms)

Step 3 Only me?   **Step 3** Others too?

Step 4 Clarify observed behaviour   Collaborate on a solution
(specific evidence for feedback)

Step 5 Possible causes?

Step 6 Prepare feedback
(including mental rehearsal)

Step 7 Give feedback and agree action

Step 1 – What is the problem?

The first step is to evaluate the problem. At this stage the problem may be expressed in general terms, for example: 'She is often very aggressive with me' or 'He seems unwilling to offer me any help when I need it'.

Step 2 – What is the evidence?

Here we look at specific instances where the problem has occurred. How often? Only in particular situations (perhaps when you are alone or only when in groups)? Based on a closer look at the evidence, you then might redefine the problem.

Step 3 – Only me? Others too?

Sometimes when we have problems with a particular person we can feel that we are the only person who feels this way. Sometimes it is very clear when you are not. At other times it is less clear and you can dig a very big hole for yourself by transposing everything back to yourself.

If it's a shared issue then you can collaborate on a solution. The steps now continue with the assumption that this is a personal issue.

Step 4 – Clarify observed behaviour

These examples should be specific and not based on hearsay or vague personality issues, so you should not say 'You're just really aggressive all the time'. You may quickly end up in a 'No, I'm not, yes you are' type discussion. Instead, you need to identify examples of when a person behaved aggressively to you.

Step 5 – Possible causes?

There are often specific reasons why difficult people behave in the way they do. Clearly if their difficult behaviour is only with you you need to look at why this is the case from the other person's point of view. Perhaps they don't like you or you lack credibility in their eyes. You also need to be honest with yourself – are there things you have done that might have triggered this behaviour? Think through this carefully because the other person may well bring things up about you to counter your feedback. Do however, keep an open mind and don't let any preconceived view prejudice any future discussion.

Step 6 – Prepare feedback

Feedback is only useful where you are able to use specific examples to support what you are saying. Have these examples ready (see step 4). Your mental rehearsal needs to be clear too:

> 'This could be a tough conversation but I have prepared for it. While they have the right to defend their actions I have the right too to say why I think their behaviour is not appropriate. I have prepared properly. This could be difficult but I can deal with this. I must stick to the facts and control my emotions even if they bring in other issues or they can't control their own emotions.'

Step 7 – Give feedback and agree action

The feedback must be evidence-based and should include a statement about the effects of the behaviour on you/the group.

> 'John/Jane, I want to talk with you about something and it might not be an easy conversation for either of us. There have been a few instances when I have felt particularly uncomfortable with you recently. For example,

the other day when you said/did "abc" it made me feel "xyz". On another occasion when you said "def" it also made me feel "xyz". I do feel that, for whatever reason, you don't seem as willing to offer help to me as you do to other people.'

Don't find excuses for the other person. Even though you will have your own view as to why the other person is behaving in a particular way (see step 5) you should let the other person draw their own conclusions.

Don't expect an immediate reaction (but you might get an immediate emotional one). If the reaction is emotional then let the emotions blow out – don't interject, for example, if the other person is angry or tearful and showing it. You could make it worse. The emotional reaction will be less common, fortunately, than a professional one.

Aim for agreement for action. But, just as you might want to think things through when you get feedback before committing, you should allow the other person to do this too. In Luck Factor 18 'Influencing' there is a worked example of this seven-step process based on a perceived lack of credibility.

Behaviour breeds behaviour – summary

- Remember that the world comprises seven billion unique and interesting personalities (that doesn't mean you have to like them all) rather than a few generic stereotypes.

- Use committed listening and questioning to understand the internal 'worlds' of other people.

- There are just a few people in life with whom, no matter what you do, you just cannot get along. Don't worry about it. Use your remaining energy to work around them.

- There is a larger group (an arbitrary 15 per cent of those you come across) with whom, if you are prepared to work at it, you can develop a productive relationship – even if you're not exactly friends.

- Use the seven-step process to help you resolve problems that you have with the behaviour of specific people.

LUCK FACTOR 17 – NETWORKING

'Networking is a pleasure for me.' ADAM

There are many myths about networking. The traditional image of the successful networker 'working the room', 'pressing the flesh' and eyeing people who can be useful to them has given networking a bad name.

In recent years, the concept of networking has changed. Three key factors have influenced this:

- The twenty-first century networker is a relationship 'builder' rather than a people 'user'.

- The advent of personalised network management tools such as LinkedIn has created an additional dimension to networking. These tools are as active or passive as you want them to be.

- If you work in hierarchical organisations your success will in part depend on working outside the traditional up–down structure. Modern thinking organisations are flatter and so the need to build relationships through networking has never been greater.

The listening and questioning skills discussed in the previous Luck Factor are a vital element to being a great networker when face to face. However, our main focus here is to look at the qualities required of you as a networker – a sort of philosophical base from which to start. This Luck Factor also uses the SID model from Luck Factor 8 to encourage you to be a proactive networker in a social situation, if this is something that doesn't sit easily with you (though you may of course be great at it).

The qualities of networkers

Great networkers share some key qualities, which we'll look at now, combined with comments from Adam who, as a formidable networker, has some sharp observations about what networking means to him and how he goes about it.

Your attitude to people

There are 'users' of people and there are those who operate on an open, mutually supportive basis. Networkers are not users. Networkers know the value of developing relationships for the long term – where a relationship begins with no expectation of what you get from it personally.

Understanding the benefits

There are unique opportunities to generate mutually supportive, long-term relationships that *may* benefit you and *may* individually benefit those in your network. There are no individual guarantees (and you should not expect there to be so). But, those who successfully create networks appreciate the overall return from their investment in people that networking requires. For Adam, the benefits relate to his love (and workplace need) for creativity:

> *'Why I think it is critical for success is that on one level it is a numbers game. So, when you have a really large network of people and you use your imagination the mathematics are such that you might well ask the right person the right question at the right time, you might well make the right connection in people terms or in ideas terms. Creativity to me is very much about* con-nections – *connections between ideas and connections between people. I see spotting and seizing opportunities as a form of creativity. You want to maximise the chances of interesting connections happening and opportunities opening up.'*

There can also be an altruistic element to this, which again Adam expresses well:

> *'What I like above all is to bring previously unconnected people together, and they usually benefit in the process – networking is a bit like matchmaking. One of the few things I remember from my degree was reading the Surrealist Manifesto by André Breton where he talks about surprising, exciting connections – he taught me a lifelong message: really powerful ideas come from bringing together two previously unconnected things. Like electricity, the bigger the potential difference, the bigger the spark.'*

Action centred

How willing are you to actively invest time in nurturing your network? This includes investing time to help people when there is no obvious or immediate benefit to you. A successful networker understands that planning and careful investment in people is more likely to be of benefit in the future. The successful networker focuses on being a long-term builder of relationships rather than a short-term user of people.

Organised

A good networker has a clear sense of the different kinds of networking relationships there are – some are close contacts in mutually supportive relationships, others are more distant but where an offer of help (by the networker) should always be possible.

Communicative

Are you interested in the worlds and lives of colleagues, contacts and friends? Utilising the questioning and listening skills from the previous Luck Factor are central here. Some of us have to work at our communication skills. As Adam says, he has had to do this himself and he has done it by observation:

> 'Networking is a pleasure for me. I am not naturally the most outgoing person but I have changed a lot since my twenties and part of that comes from being married to someone who is a natural born communicator and watching how she thrives on people and their stories.'

Socially proactive

A good networker makes an active effort to talk with people in social situations. This is one of the toughest parts – some people really find it difficult to 'circulate' at things like industry events and other social occasions. Walking into a room of 200 people, where you know very few of them, and making conversation can be difficult. We'll look at this in more detail below and see how SID (Luck Factor 8) can help you in this situation.

A good maintainer

Good networkers make a conscious effort to keep their network up-to-date and, when they have an opportunity to get in touch with their contacts, they do so. This quote from Adam is a very illustrative example of what maintenance means:

> *'I really feel it is important not to let inertia get in the way of friendships and relationships. I might not see someone for two or three years, but I don't let that stop me picking up with them when the opportunity presents itself and I always take the chance to maintain the connection when I can. It's good and enjoyable to nurture your network, to really enjoy the encounters and connections – good things constantly come out of it.'*

Being socially proactive

Networking at conferences and large meetings and annual company get-togethers can be a valuable source of contacts but it can also make some people uneasy. Walking into a room and engaging strangers in conversation comes naturally to a few of us but rather more than a few of us don't really know how to start. Using SID (your sound inner dialogue) provides a method for getting mentally prepared for this situation. SID has six steps and we shall use these as our preparation base, as outlined here, together with possible responses to these six steps:

Step 1 – The situation (S)

Identify the difficult situation you foresee:

'Engaging strangers in conversation.'

Step 2 – The specifics (S)

What is it specifically that you are uncomfortable with about this situation?

'Making an introduction with impact – I don't really know how to start. People won't be interested in talking with me. I could get stuck with someone boring!'

Step 3 – The significance (S)

It is important that you understand how your feelings about this situation impact on your behaviour. Nervous about something? What are the likely effects of those nerves?

'My behaviour will reflect what's going on inside me. I may be reticent when I introduce myself. Perhaps the words won't come out as clearly as I would like. I might struggle to think of things to say.'

Step 4 – The implications (I)

A dose of realism is needed. First, is the worst-case scenario likely to occur anyway? Second, you need to understand that the previously identified impact on your behaviour is likely to create the very situation you had anticipated. In other words it plays out as a self-fulfilling prophecy.

> *'I can see that if I am not comfortable about this that my behaviour – unclear voice, lack of eye contact – will reflect this. In that sense it will be self-fulfilling.'*

Step 5 – The investigation (I)

The investigation injects a dose of reality and flips the negative feelings into a positive frame of mind. You start with the following questions:

- 'Has this ever happened to me before?'

  'Well, I have found these situations very difficult at first and I do end up drinking a bit too much to get through it.'

- 'Am I looking at the worst-case scenario and playing this as though this is likely to happen every time?'

  'Well, I suppose I have had a mix of experiences. Once or twice I have got talking to someone really interesting and really enjoyed it. Other times I have been bored with people or, at other times I suspect people have wanted to get away from me. So, I shouldn't see this as something that is always bad for me.'

So here you bring balance into your inner dialogue. You then address the specific points you raised in step 2:

■ *'Making an introduction with impact – I don't really know how to start.'* My suggestions for doing this include the following:

– People start to form an impression of you in the first 5–30 seconds of contact. It can be hard to shake that initial impression off, even if it's entirely false – consider therefore the image you want to project.

– 'Telescope' your handshake by holding your arm/hand out as you walk towards someone. Thrusting your hand out when right in front of the other person can come as a surprise. Give a good confident shake but don't overdo it. Make a point of remembering the other person's name and use it as soon as possible.

– Say 'I am [name]' and briefly (just a few words) what you do. Using the words 'I am' confidently attaches importance to you. Saying the first few words clearly helps to get rid of inner tension.

– Then switch the focus of the conversation swiftly to the other person (remembering the listening and questioning skills) – in fact, as already suggested this is a great work and life strategy. Good networkers don't talk about themselves (unless asked).

– Have some 'openers'. These are good ones for large-scale conferences and meetings: *'It feels good to get up and move about'*; *'How have you found the day, did you find something of particular interest?'*; *'What line of business are you in?'*; *'What's your interest in being here?'*

- Keep a sensible distance – don't be overfamiliar.

- Maintain eye contact but don't do an eyeball-to-eyeball stare out.

- Keep smiling if appropriate.

■ *'People won't be interested in talking with me.'* People like talking about themselves, so rather than focusing on yourself (as this statement implies) ask people about themselves. If you are really struggling to connect and you sense boredom from the other person (lack of eye contact, for example) then take the initiative yourself. A couple of suggestions appear in the next point.

■ *'I could get stuck with someone boring!'* If you were preparing for this in your own mind your inner dialogue might run along the lines of:

'I must be realistic about this. I can't expect to get on with everyone and that's just a fact of life. So – how do I get away from this person? I could close the conversation off but be very polite while doing it – "It's really good to meet you, Gary. I am going to get myself something to eat/drink etc. I am sure we will bump into each other later." And I should feel comfortable saying, "We've got each other's cards. I'm going to take the chance to meet a few other people. We'll keep in touch." They might be as relieved as me, if we're not hitting it off. I could introduce them to a colleague (just because we aren't connecting doesn't mean others won't connect with them) or, if there's a bigger conversation going on, say something like "That looks interesting, shall we see what's going on over there?"'

Note: it's good to remember that even if you do hit it off, you should not spend all your time with the same person.

Step 6 – Dynamism (D)

'OK, I am ready to have a go. I think it's probably a lot to do with my own attitude to this. What I have to be is confident in myself and send out a signal to other people that I want to talk to them. If I get bored or I sense they are bored I have a strategy to get away without offending anyone. Actually, even though I am a bit nervous, I am looking forward to this.'

Networking – summary

- Make the other person's world the centre of yours.
- Use good listening and questioning skills to do this.
- Be a relationship builder rather than a relationship user – invest in people even if there is no obvious benefit to you.
- Maintain your network of contacts – don't let contacts 'drop'.
- Be proactive with increasing your network of contacts.
- Keep a confident 'up' voice (even if you don't feel confident) at networking events. Ask people about themselves – resist the temptation to talk about yourself.

LUCK FACTOR 18 – INFLUENCING

When you look at your job you can probably clearly see those areas of it over which you have control. But it's harder to identify the areas over which you have influence.

It is likely that the difference between the two is that where we have control people are less likely to be involved and where we perceive influence the 'people factor' is likely to be paramount.

Influencing is a state of mind. Take two people doing the same or similar jobs (perhaps one of them could be you?). Their perception of the level of influence they have may be very different. The answer to the question 'How much influence do you have in your job?' can only be answered subjectively and can only be based on the way you treat those over whom you want to have influence.

Think carefully about this. First, consider those over whom you have a degree of influence at the moment. Then, think carefully about the people over whom you would *like* to have influence but at the moment don't think you do. The gap could be big or small depending on your knowledge and skills as an influencer.

While you can have influence through the flexing of an obvious source of power – being a team captain or a manager, for example – if you have to remind people of this power source then you immediately lose the credibility that the softer sources of influence (such as trust and credibility) give you. Many of us don't have these overt sources of power anyway and depend on the softer methods.

You get results through people and not despite them. If you recognise that success comes quickest to those who invest time in building better relationships – even with those you don't necessarily get on with – you will find that people will naturally do things for and with you when there may be no compelling reason for them to do so. Because you are 'you' they *want* to do this.

This is not in any way about manipulation. It is a much more natural, organic process than that. And it usually takes time to get there. This comes through the exercising of influence. And to be able to influence you need to build trust and credibility.

Having influence through trust and credibility gives you this 'soft' power. There are other ways to influence in particular situations – a manager can do so through the authority vested in the managerial role, for example. However, the soft sources are universally accessible to everyone, regardless of who you are and whether you are able to exercise 'hard' power at all.

Quick fixes are often superficial but there are some effective ways to build both trust and your credibility quickly:

- Make other people look good – help them deliver in their own roles. Even if they are not inclined to give credit, people do notice who provides the 'glue'.

- Make yourself invaluable by doing that extra bit that turns OK into excellent. The attention to detail mentioned in Chapter 4 'Performing' applies here.

- Don't let anyone sense that you are easily sidetracked. In the office that means no Facebook, checking private emails and non-work-related web surfing. Be professional.

These tips will build on your influence, but you need to sustain them – people quickly forget a favour or the hard work on a previous project.

Trust

Sometimes quick fixes are not enough and you just have to invest time in something to make it work for you. Gaining trust is not an overnight activity. If you have to say 'Trust me' you are likely to lose trust as a source of influence. Others will decide whether they trust you or not. It is up to you and me to give ourselves the best chance of people trusting us. Here are some suggestions for building that trust (this is a short list because some of the building trust issues are shared with 'credibility' in the next section):

- **Consistency**. This isn't necessarily about being consistently 'nice'. To look at this from the opposite perspective, it can be tough to deal with a challenging perfectionist, but if this person is consistently like this then at least we know what the expectation is and can respond accordingly.

- **Reliability**. You do what you say you are going to do, and do it to a particular standard.

- **Honesty**. You say what you think and feel but in such a way that respects another person's right to be addressed in an appropriate manner.

- **'We' not 'me'**. For example, you don't take the credit for team successes yourself.

- **Equality**. Wherever you are and whoever you are, treating people with respect and dignity should be part of you.

Credibility

Your reputation – and by reputation I mean a good one – is based on your credibility. But what gives you credibility in one sphere may not in another, so there is an intuitive side to this. As with trust, it will take time to build credibility and this requires the interpersonal skills that have featured earlier in this chapter.

Your reputation will be based on what is valued by those around you. That in turn might be based on things like age, experience, qualifications and previous successes. However, I do believe that over the next 20 years people will be less and less willing to accord respect based on formal qualifications. With a huge number of people now having degrees (in developed countries between 30 and 50 per cent of young people will go to university over the next ten years) what used to differentiate people has now become the norm. So, people will be asking 'OK, but what can you do?' Or, more likely 'OK, but what can you do that's different and better than others?' If you have recently graduated, the degree gets you to the door, but once the door is opened, unless the degree is highly vocational (which 95 per cent are not), it counts for little.

If you want to build a good reputation then work out what is valued by those around you – particularly around your interpersonal skills. This could be a cultural issue. But here I refer particularly to group culture – sports teams, work teams and so on – as much as national or regional cultures. Some groups value consensual, collaborative approaches. Other groups prefer a leader to give out instructions and then follow. In some team cultures an open, forthright communication style is valued. In others much higher levels of diplomacy might be needed. But ultimately your reputation will grow if you are seen to get results and not wind people up in the process.

So, those are just a few of the factors that give you credibility. Here is a more extensive list:

- **Your age and experience**. In traditional environments these are valued above all else. Of course, you can't change these two things if you are under 30. But what you can do, without being sycophantic and regardless of your personal view of their competence, is to accord respect to those who have these two things. It will provide a solid base from which you develop your relationship with those who are older. You will need these people 'onside' on your way up.

- **Your results**. There's nothing like results for getting credibility. Perhaps the best piece of advice I have heard on this is to always remember to focus on the end result first and then worry about the process: 'Where do I want to get to?' followed by 'How am I going to get there?' People who don't deliver often get this the wrong way round.

- **Managing relationships**. Although getting results is so important, this has to be done within the framework of maintaining good relationships. Task and people go together. In fact, if you manage your relationships in the right way the task becomes easier. If hell really is other people then the problem is you, not other people. We do hear about the odd task-driven 'bastard' who tramples over people to succeed. And succeed they sometimes do. We don't hear about the many more people who use this approach and who fail miserably.

- **Brain before mouth**. You may know a few people who are mouth first and brain afterwards. Think things through carefully before you engage your vocal parts. And if you are thinking off the top of your head then be very clear that this is what you are doing – people will cut you a bit of slack rather than think that you don't know what you are talking about. Everyone knows the blagger apart from blaggers themselves.

- **Qualifications**. To recap a point in the introduction to this section – qualifications can help you get to a certain point but if everyone has them then what's going to put you in a different place? In other parts of this book I have mentioned your individuality and said how important that can be. What's even more important are the people skills that some of us pick up when growing up – working in teams and groups, negotiating, influencing, listening, questioning and collaborating – which we are rarely formally taught. These are the skills that will set you apart.

What to do if someone doesn't think you have credibility

In Luck Factor 16 I introduced a seven-stage process for dealing with a difficult person. We are now going to use that model as a means of dealing with a common situation: 'What do I do if I think someone feels I lack credibility?' I have picked this for a very good reason. Over the last ten years I have run more than 100 one- and two-day seminars on communication skills. During those seminars

I usually run an improvised session where we look at different communication issues anonymously brought up by participants. This issue of lack of credibility comes up far more than anything else.

I have invented a person, Sue, who has the credibility issue with someone else. Here is an inner dialogue that 'someone else' might have as they prepare to deal with the issue:

Step 1 – What is the problem? 'Sue doesn't think I have much credibility.'

Step 2 – What is the evidence? 'She talks over me in meetings, she always challenges my opinion and when we discuss anything in meetings she won't make eye contact. Actually, if I look closely at this it seems that it happens when we are with other people – particularly at our team meetings. So perhaps I should think of this as a problem with her taking me and my thoughts seriously in front of others. But I think the credibility issue is important here.'

Step 3 – Only me? Others too? 'It does seem to be only me. My boss isn't the sort of person who can or will deal with this, so I either drop it or sort it out myself.'

Step 4 – Clarify observed behaviour. 'A few instances. Last week when we had a brainstorming there were two specific instances when she shot my ideas down before I had barely finished expressing them. Another time I was presenting some data and she talked right over what I was saying. I felt that she had barely noticed I was speaking.'

Step 5 – Possible causes? 'I am quite new – perhaps she respects experience. Maybe she sees me as a threat too? I could easily be wrong and I should keep an open mind.'

Step 6 – Prepare feedback. 'She is quite a tough character so I should be prepared for a difficult conversation. I have the right to bring this up but she has the right to defend herself and be listened to. But I do have specific examples that I can use and I should also let her know how her behaviour affects me. It might not be easy but she takes her work seriously and I am sure she will be as concerned as I am about this. She might not be of course. But even if she isn't, I must let her know that I am unhappy. I should let her deal with this in her own way.'

Step 7 – Give feedback. 'Hello, Sue. This might not be easy for either of us but I want to talk with you about something that I'm struggling with. There have been a few instances where, for whatever reason, you seem not to have been taking my inputs into team discussions seriously. If I can give you a couple of examples ...'

These kinds of discussions are not the easiest. But a clearly thought out plan works wonders. In fact, if you were involved in this kind of conversation for real you might find you get credibility quite quickly – you are prepared to deal with important issues when they arise and do not shy away from what needs to be said/done.

Influencing – summary

- Your sphere of influence is as big or small as you perceive it to be.

- People will be more willing to be influenced by you if they trust you and you are credible.

- Both trust and credibility are built over time, which can be frustrating.

- Building trust requires consistency, reliability and treating people as equals.

- Your credibility will be based on your skills, knowledge and experience and your previous successes.

- Culture (group, team, regional, national) plays an important part in how credible people think you are – what the prevailing culture thinks is important.

- Don't remind people of your sources of influence ('You can trust me'). You lose its effectiveness as a source if you have to do this.

THE LUCK FACTOR 19 – SHARING SUCCESS

'In the sailing team if we won a race things like "high-fiving" were out. It was get the boat back, put every-thing away, nice and controlled, and then a race to the bar to drink huge amounts of alcohol. I found that emo-tionally constipated. Now, when I am with the team, I encourage them to celebrate success right away. Get the feeling out. I tell them that with our success will come relationships with each other that will last for the rest of our lives. It's important to be open with our feel-ings. I watch myself winning gold in 1992 and I didn't really know how to celebrate.' GREG

This, the shortest of the Luck Factors, is about 'atmosphere' – between you and others – and three very simple things you can do to create a better one.

Giving praise and thanking people are the first two things and should be done because you want to do it. People see lack of sincerity straight away. But a benefit is that we always remember the people best who take the time to remember us and you are probably no different. This is why the acknowledgement of what people do for you – through praise and thanks – is so important.

The third simple thing you can do is to celebrate success.

Praise

Luck Factor 6 talked about receiving feedback and its importance in learning. The focus was more on feedback given when there is room for improvement. However, praise is also a form of feedback and something you can give freely – when deserved. In working environments it's sometimes assumed that this is something that only managers do. But it is of course our individual responsibility to manage our relationships. So remember to:

- **Praise the effort**. When you reflect on something you did well you probably remember the feeling as much as the mechanics around the thing you did well. 'That was hard work', 'I had to really concentrate to get that done', are the sorts of things we say to ourselves after a tough task, well done. Other people will feel the same. So 'I know the amount of effort you put in', or 'I know when I do something like that, how tough I find it' are good phrases to use when you praise other people.

- **Look for specifics**. Let people know what you like about what they did. Think about how it feels when you get told 'Well done' – you probably want to know what was 'well done' about what you did.

Thanks

Another way to strengthen relationships and to show that you've noticed is to say 'Thanks'. No matter what the environment, it's healthy to acknowledge what people have done for you. I make this admittedly obvious point because I know how rare thanks can be. I am often appalled, for example, by the attitude of footballers who score a goal and run off in celebration and to receive adulation and even exultant audience worship. Sometimes there is a complete lack of recognition by the new hero-figure for the player who made the great break or supplied the killer pass.

We forget to give thanks every day in long-term relationships and marriages where the familiarity means we cut corners in the time we give to each other. And we see it too at work where, for a number of reasons, including a perceived lack of time or the 'move-on' mentality that pitches us from one project to the next, human kindnesses such as 'thank yous' get forgotten.

I think two things are responsible for this:

- **Outsize ego**. *'You are here to do this for me and you are doing what you are meant to be doing.'* This view comes from the person who sees themself as the sun at the centre of the solar system around which everything revolves.

- **Taking for granted**. The longer we spend around people – work colleagues, sports teams, hobby groups, friends, partners – the easier it can be to take them for granted. This is a habit that is easy to slip into and a sign perhaps that we have ceased to be sensitised to the needs of others.

As with praise, a thank-you costs nothing and, as long as it sincere, is a simple valuable way of strengthening a bond. The receiver will be glad that you have taken the time to thank them and you will know how they feel because you know how you feel when it is done to you.

Success

Sit through a two-hour meeting at work and analyse what's being discussed. It seems that meetings are often little more than problem-solving discussions. Sports teams, when they analyse the last match, will look at the things that they didn't do well rather than what worked.

Imagine for a moment spinning this on its head and looking at what's gone well rather than what hasn't – the things you did right. Of course we have to learn from our mistakes, but it's very motivating also to reflect on and learn from our successes.

Suspend your own ego – show an appreciation of the success of others. Be spontaneous and be genuine. It will be particularly powerful if you had no personal investment in the success. Don't take the praise for other's successes.

The quickest way to create the next success is to really know how it feels and what it means to have had the last one. You want more.

And, if it's a personal success …

In Luck Factor 15 I referred to psychologist Martin Seligman's idea of remembering three simple pleasures from the day before you go to sleep. There's no reason why once in a while the simple pleasures can't be three small successes.

Sharing success – summary

- Praise and thanks cost nothing except a small amount of time.
- Praise and thanks create a positive atmosphere – people love to be remembered.
- Be sincere.
- Be specific.
- Remember the good stuff you do and not just the problems.

CHAPTER 7

Opportunity

'Opportunity is what it's all about and being exposed to all the kinds of things you can do. I go to talk at certain schools and I realise that these kids have never been taught that there's this thing called creativity that you can do all kinds of things with.' JOHN HEGARTY, advertising guru and champion of open-minded thinking

Luck Factor in this chapter:

Luck Factor 20 – Spotting opportunities

Opportunities exist all around us but most of the time they lie hidden under the demands of everyday living, which blind us to the almost endless possibilities that life offers. An obvious but pertinent metaphor for this is to think about how much we love that 'wow' feeling when we look out of an aeroplane window on a clear day and see the Earth spread below us. Our imagination fires away as we think about the millions of things our fellow citizens could be doing below. However, that feeling soon dissipates when we arrive at the airport and have to engage in the hassle of customs clearance and luggage collection, not to mention the journey to the hotel or home afterwards. In a world of opportunities we become locked into the minutiae of everyday living and tune ourselves out of possibility.

Somewhere, if you trace your steps back, everything you do now stems from an opportunity you spotted to do something new or different. You applied for the job, took up a new hobby, had a eureka moment that fired your imagination to do something, or maybe – going a long way back – you joined a club at school that started a life-long interest in something. What you did was spot, and then take, an opportunity.

The Luck Habit has its genesis in opportunity spotting where you pitch reaction against anticipation – or what I call our infinite search engine capacity. By that I mean your ability as a human being to identify opportunity anywhere and at any time – against your 'doctor' tendency. We usually only go to a doctor when we feel unwell, i.e. when there's an obvious problem. In the same way those who don't have the Luck Habit tend to act only when there is the need to react – and maybe not even then. In contrast, those with the Luck Habit act when there may be no compelling reason to do so. There is no big problem or crisis, but their default mode is to *think* (that sound inner dialogue again) and *act* affirmatively, problem/crisis or not. I could easily have called this chapter 'Luck spotting'.

LUCK FACTOR 20 – SPOTTING OPPORTUNITIES

Parts of this book have assumed that you want to perform better at something you already do. However, you may be reading this book because you want to start something afresh and then get better at it. In this chapter we look at how you can spot opportunities to help get you started. I've divided it into three parts:

- **Priming**. Putting yourself into a state of preparedness to spot and take the opportunities that exist – the right psychological base.

- **Creating**. Making a conscious effort to create opportunities through imagination – yours and others.

- **Playing**. What happens when you take an opportunity and act on it?

PRIMING

The more you put yourself in a position where opportunities are likely to occur, the more likely you are to spot them. A wider range of experiences and engagements with your world 'primes' your brain to identify new possibilities. We have developed a whole range of sayings to support this, such as 'The early bird catches the worm' and 'Fortune favours the brave'.

What is likely to happen is that your brain enjoys the stimulus of the initial experience and is therefore more highly tuned into the same or similar stimulus if it occurs again.

These stimuli can happen by accident and sometimes when we least expect them. You may find that you enjoy a night out more when you were resistant to the idea of going out in the first place ('A pleasant surprise') than you did the long-anticipated party. However, for most of us, most of the time, we need to get out there, stimulate our brain and enjoy more first-time and re-energising experiences.

If you want to be an opportunity-spotter (or taker), priming your brain – sensitising it to a massive world of possibility – is important. There are three skills that help get you into a state of preparedness for opportunity spotting:

Omnipresence

We get told that opportunities exist everywhere. And they do. The challenge is to loosen your thinking sufficiently to spot them.

Writer Roger von Oech talks of the explorer approach to spotting opportunities. The explorer looks round corners as well as straight ahead because there might be something a little more interesting in the less obvious places. In the questionnaire in Chapter 1 I used a couple of metaphorical questions to make this point. One of them asked if you ever look up when walking down the street or if you keep your gaze at eye-level. It's amazing what you see if you look up. One of my neighbours had no idea that the row of old houses that we live in was built in 1856 because she'd never noticed the plaque high on the wall on the side of one of the houses at the end of the street which would tell her this (it's not like it's a long street – only six houses). So the lesson here is: 'Widen your gaze' – and there are an unlimited number of places to look.

Creativity writer Mark Brown talks of opportunities like 'white light' – omnipresent in the same way that opportunities are. I like to think of opportunities in the way we think of a web search engine. A single word typed into a search engine generates a huge number – sometimes millions – of possibilities. The first couple of pages generally give practical and logical links based on your request. But sometimes the most interesting responses come on pages 8, 9, 10 and beyond. The questionnaire in Chapter 1 asked about this. Do you as a matter of course only look at the first page of links or do you go beyond that? If you go beyond you will notice that the links on subsequent pages interpret your search criteria in quite interesting ways. There's always a little gem of a website there if you're prepared to look – a new discovery. This is really about being curious – looking a bit further and a bit harder than others to see what they can't see. As writer, humourist and critic Dorothy Parker once said: 'The best cure for boredom is curiosity. There is no cure for curiosity.'

You can also think about opportunities in the way that Big Bang theorists talk about the Universe (including up to one septillion stars). The Universe emerged from what's called a 'singularity' – a 'thing' infinitesimally, unimaginably small (a billionth the size of a proton). The Big Bang still goes on now, 13.7 billion years later. The comparison with your opportunities here is that once an initial opportunity is conceived and then taken up by you there really is no limit on where that opportunity can take you. It's your very own big bang. Everything changes forever.

Barrier demolition

'I will always love flying – I fought too hard to become an airline pilot to fall out of love with it. But I love opportunity too and I always have half an eye on what's going on around me. I think that taking the chances I had to be a pilot when I was young has made me a bit more sensitive to any opportunities that exist for me now. I got married about three years ago and as part of my wedding I decided to offer specially made sweets for wedding guests. Not long after that I started getting calls – can you do this for my wedding? And along with an old school friend, Sarah, we saw a great opportunity to offer confectionery for special occasions. The business is going well and we are currently planning to open our first retail outlet in Dublin. Just because I am an airline pilot doesn't mean I am only an airline pilot. There are so many other things I can do and I think that I must try at least some of them.' BERNICE

Opportunities are not manufactured, but they do present themselves best to those who are able to sense the energising potential of new situations. I have already mentioned Helene who took up singing at the age of 67 and now travels the world with the Royal Philharmonic Choir; I also know of a Mexican street-fighting revolutionary who ended up as a leading professor at a top American university, and a charity worker who climbed the seven highest peaks of the world's seven continents. They are many stories like this and no doubt you have some of your own. People for whom opportunities opened up because they took a step in a different, previously unexplored direction.

There are four barriers that need to be broken down to be a great opportunity spotter (and taker):

- Inaccurate self-perception.
- The idea that opportunities exist only for certain kinds of people.
- An attitude of 'I am right and I can prove it' – stuckness.
- Poor reasoning.

As with so much in the Luck Habit the starting point is self-awareness. So many people suffer from a lack of self-awareness and become prisoners of their own self-perception. As a result they either don't see opportunities that could be right for them or take opportunities that are not right.

Traps can exist everywhere – for example, do you define yourself by the job that you currently do? Bernice's quote is so apt here – just because she is an airline pilot doesn't mean that she cannot also run a specialist business providing confectionery for special events. Sometimes we hear unemployed people rigidly describing themselves as an unemployed … (fill in the gap: lorry driver, insurance salesperson) with the implication that this is what they do to the exclusion of all else.

If acquiring the Luck Habit is about your interpretation of your world and the influences on it, most importantly yourself, then this interpretation requires a healthy dose of self-understanding. By 'healthy' I mean an appreciation of yourself that stops short of turning analysis into stasis.

Not only do we make assumptions about ourselves, we also do this about specific opportunities. If you make assumptions about, say, entrepreneurs (extrovert, bursting with ideas) you will discount yourself if you don't have these characteristics. There are many introverted entrepreneurs and many who are very skilled at developing the ideas of others rather than creating them personally.

You and I have a bias towards confirmation of currently held views and opinions. We look for the signs and signals that confirm what we already believe to be true and ignore the things that don't conform. This creates a degree of stuckness – a self-perpetuating cycle of living in which we only see what we want to see.

Have you ever heard the old saying: 'When everything changes you go back to zero'? A further barrier is that we fail to notice when our skills have become outdated or when, if you work in the private sector, you are so blinded by the success of the business you work for that you fail to notice the new upstart on the block who is redefining the way your industry sector will operate in the future. Stuckness also exists as 'The way I/we do it'.

An art-house film I saw a few years ago (*Kandahar*) told the story of the progress of a young woman across Iran and Afghanistan as she travels to reach her sister in Kandahar. At one point, amidst the unceasing grimness, a gloriously optimistic young man says: 'Yes, but when the walls are high, the sky is even higher'.

Recognising the almost complete lack of opportunity in Afghanistan ('the walls') sensitised him to all the opportunities that exist elsewhere ('the sky'). It's why so many of the great American opportunity-takers of the late nineteenth and early twentieth century were not from America at all. And, as a further thought, why do so many of us who live in the sky – the land of opportunity – choose to build a wall in it?

Scrapping

In the future we may look at the 50 years up to 2010 as some sort of unreality rather than the normality we've come to accept. In most western societies we've had good healthcare, free education, state pensions, social security, easy credit, good homes and a car. With the odd exception, we've enjoyed the cradle-to-grave provision championed by social reformers. At the time of writing things are not looking so straightforward. Indeed we may never go back to those 'fur-lined' days.

The cosy assumptions we've made about our lives are being challenged. Some of those assumptions may be scaled down or even disappear (pensions, for example). This is a frightening thought for some of us, yet to all previous generations the 'soft landing' we've enjoyed never existed. They had to scrap and hustle, and deal with uncertainty. They needed all the wonderful human traits of ideas, improvisation and ingenuity to survive. They had to be self-sufficient.

You might not feel comfortable with the idea that the soft three-ply quilted toilet tissue that is modern-day living may be replaced by sandpaper. It probably won't be. But those old scrapping skills that served previous generations so well are needed now in a way they haven't been for many years. We need to be primed to spot and make the most of our opportunities. It could be the making of us. It could be the making of you. Never was the Luck Habit needed more.

So, a good step in priming yourself for opportunity is to be prepared to think more by your wits, respond to ambiguity and adversity and improvise when the opportunities are a bit different from the ones you imagined.

Priming – summary

- Adversity (which we might see more of over the next few years) demands more sensitivity to spot opportunities and imagination to create them.

- Opportunities exist everywhere – can you put yourself psychologically (or physically) in a place where you are able to see them?

- You will 'see' only as far as you choose to 'see'.

- Don't place false barriers (such as your perceived lack of knowledge, skills and suitability) between yourself and the opportunities of the future. There are opportunities for all kinds of personalities and people.

- Keep your skills updated.

- Ask: 'Who's doing things that are fundamentally different from the way I/we currently do things? Who's challenging the status quo and how are they doing it?'

CREATING

Opportunity spotting is a form of creativity and this section looks at three ways you can create opportunities. They follow on from the priming tools (and some of them overlap).

Practice

This sits very well with the chapters on learning and performance where I championed the value of practice with purpose. The better you get at something, the more opportunities seem to open up for you to get even better. And, assuming you do improve, the more you see ways in which you can use your improved performance in opportunistic ways. Think about Gates, Jobs and others, who in the 1970s immersed themselves totally in computer technology in their garages or bedrooms or kitchens to a point where their hours and hours of practice with these technologies allowed them to fashion the future. An extreme example, but it makes the point that persistent, purposeful practice leads to mastery and further opportunity.

Very little happens to those who do nothing.

Collaboration

Since 1800 the world has lived with the 'great man' theory of creation. It's not so difficult to see why. Those readers with a religion are likely to see the ultimate creator as a single male entity. Christianity has taken the 'great man' theory to an extreme, where the creator also comes with a full beard for additional male authenticity. Nineteenth-century technological leaps had men like Alexander

Graham Bell, Isambard Kingdom Brunel and Thomas Edison as their genitors. In the following century and a bit we have continued this notion that great ideas, whether they were hatched to solve problems or make the most of opportunities, come from individual eureka moments – although twentieth-century emancipation has meant that the freedom to have great ideas (and act on them) is not gender-specific.

However, a quick look at patents around the world suggests that these moments of individual inspiration are not the norm. In fact, relying on them to solve problems or ferment opportunities is an extremely unreliable way to move from A to B. Great when they happen, but not so good as an easy-to-access resource in times of trouble. The inspired solution may arrive. But it probably won't.

Great ideas usually come about as a result of collaborative processes and they need time to be nurtured into something of real value. It might be one person who acts, but the idea or the opportunity is hatched through the coming together of layer upon layer of thinking on an idea. The opportunity becomes less a random thought and more a tangible solution that one person, or more likely a group of people, will act on. So, although this book has a 'you'–centred tone, using the art of collaboration as a way of developing your own ideas or using the random thoughts of others (without stealing of course) to hatch your own opportunities are real skills. If you're working on new opportunities as part of a group, the following points are important:

- **Notice**. Give people time to think – don't expect instant answers. As has been seen in this book already, not only should you give yourself time to think but you should also give others time as well.

- **Outsiders**. At least some of the people you collaborate with should be people who can give a different perspective.

- **Share the goal**. Collaborate with those who share your motivation to create. This motivation can come through a personal identification with the goal or a willingness to help.

- **Never be satisfied**. Don't take an idea at face value. Can you tighten it up, be more specific? Ask the question 'What else?' and then ask it again until you have exhausted all avenues. The power of a number of minds on this will strengthen the idea development/improvement process.

- **Be open**. Welcome the ideas of others and be genuine about it. Avoid criticism of the ideas people have – they'll soon stop having them.

- **Acknowledge contribution**. Don't steal. No one wants to work or play with people who don't give credit when it's due.

Celestial thoughts

A classic old saying says that if you aim for stars you may hit the Moon. If you aim for the Moon you may not make it out of the Earth's atmosphere. Here is an example of that from Michele:

'In the early 1990s computers started to be commonplace in offices and computer skills became a necessity if you wanted to work in an office. I had been working with different groups providing training for people who would

otherwise not have been able to afford training. Women returners to work, for example. Computers were very expensive for us then – we couldn't afford to buy new ones, but businesses were just throwing them away in the City of London. So I knocked on a few doors and asked if we could have the ones they didn't want any more. When Coopers and Lybrand asked "How many computers do you want?" I said "How many have you got?" I thought they might have a dozen or so. They had a thousand. The opportunity to grow a social enterprise had begun.'

Michele says it was the most entrepreneurial thing she had done up to that point. Head-based realism is important but setting your sights too low can mean missing out on a really great opportunity (in Michele's case 988 computers). And, while emotions-based motivation will raise the bar for you, perhaps even unrealistically so, you are still likely to get further than you might have done. So much of the Luck Habit is about self-fulfilling prophecy – as has been seen in other chapters. This – setting a low target – is yet another example.

There is a difference between aiming for the stars and pure fantasy. Bill Gates and Steve Jobs did not set out to create two of the world's biggest companies. And you are not going to win the 100 metres at the Olympics at the age of 80 (although you might in 200–300 years' time).

Creating – summary

- True immersion in something creates insights and possibilities you may not have seen if you hadn't got involved – provided you keep an open mind.

- Collaborate with others – collaboration often provides the propulsion for your own half-thought-out ideas.

- Aim higher – a stretch goal rather than a routine one can mean a level of attainment you might not have thought possible.

PLAYING

So, now you have primed your brain to be open to opportunity, you are aware of the barriers that get in the way and you know how to create opportunities, it's time to play with the results and make some decisions. With all these opportunities around, which ones do you take up? Which ones make sense? Which ones are right for you? Then, when you're in this new world you need to adapt to it and appreciate that once the lid's off the tin it's almost impossible to get it back on again.

'I reached a point quite early in life where I had to make a critical decision. I have been an Irish dancer for many years (I am now an instructor) and in my early twenties I got offered a part in Lord of the Dance. It was a great opportunity. But at the same time I had embarked on my training to be a pilot. I had already invested a lot of money and hard work into my training. I was, as they say, following my star. Being sensible, I realised that being a pilot provided long-term security. Lord of the Dance was short-term, but I have to say – aside from the career path – I loved flying too. I was able to follow my heart but I was also able to take the sensible option. If I hadn't loved flying so much, the decision would have gone the other way. I haven't regretted it for a moment.' BERNICE

Bernice's experience draws on two important 'playing' elements when you are at the decision-making stage:

- **The whole 'head'**. Clear, rational thinking and assessment of risk.

- **The whole 'heart'**. The emotional propulsion that drives you from idea/opportunity to action.

Whole head

In Bernice's case her head was saying 'being a pilot provided long-term security'. Jumping into anything without thinking is rarely a good idea. Clear thinking helps you ask the right kind of questions: What is experience telling me here? Who is available to help me? Where can I generate time to allow me to do this? What do I see as the benefits to me of doing this? What are the financial implications? The whole head allows obstacle clearance. The more obstacles you can clear, the easier the path to achievement will be – though 'easier' does not mean 'easy'.

Investment guru Warren Buffett once said that risk is when you don't know what you're doing. And sometimes you do have to accept that you don't and can't know everything. In fact if you need perfect information to make the perfect decision you will never have enough … and never do anything. So, there will always be risk. And, as analysts of the recent financial meltdown will attest, weaknesses will get found out. What you can do is mitigate against that risk by having a plan in place if the worst happens. A little bit of scenario planning – thinking ahead – works here.

Whole Heart

How much is your heart in your decision? This cannot be forced. It is generated in most cases by the connection or 'affinity' you feel for what you are doing (we're back to Luck Factor 1 again), though in some cases the motivators can be fuelled by external factors such as the energy generated by people around you. While rational thinking allows you to decide which path to take, the emotional element creates the necessary propulsion to start you walking down the path. The heart also does one more thing for you. It allows you to access your intuition – that sense that the path you are taking feels 'right' or 'wrong'. Intuition can be fabulously right and occasionally fabulously wrong, but it is probably as good as any hard analytical tool in decision making.

Whole … heart … head … ness

To make the right judgements you need a combination of this systematic analysis (the head) and emotional drive (the heart). This is what I call 'whole-heart-head-ness'. You need a combination of the hard and the soft to progress and make the most of the opportunities that will work best for you. You are likely to have an orientation towards one element rather than the other, but don't ignore one at the expense of the other.

The new language

Being thrust into a jazz 'supergroup', having taken up guitar relatively late in comparison to his peers, Mo saw that he was suddenly playing with musicians who were another level up from the one he was used to:

> *'I realised that I didn't speak their language. And I realised that if I was going to survive I was going to need to speak their language quickly. So I did. I adapted and learnt the language. You must learn to adapt to the new opportunity if you have to.'*

If you're with people who know more than you, you can either be intimidated by it or inspired by it. Mo has already talked about how he 'models' his learning (see Luck Factor 7) – here he extends this principle into new environments where the need is to keep up. You have to balance the need for being 'you' – the things about you that got you into the opportunity – with the adaptability needed to survive in your new environment.

This need for adaptability also hit Michele in her new circumstances. She literally did change the language she used to make the most of the opening door she had created:

> *'I needed space now. I asked my landlord if he would rent me his basement in return for a share of any profit [the landlord would become Michele's husband!]. We were now taking computers from businesses and passing them on to low-income homes but at this stage we were working with low volumes. A good company in Luton then offered us space, giving us the chance to develop what we did. At this stage I was analysing the market and I realised that I was looking at it in the wrong way. We needed to change our focus from raising funds to **selling more**.*

A simple rephrasing of her business focus from 'raising funds' to 'selling more' took the business from being a charity to being a charity with a solid, commercial outlook – but still with its core values intact. It made a big difference.

So, to summarise the two key points:

- The new language doesn't necessarily need to be some-one else's (as it was in Mo's case). It can easily be you changing the language.

- Adaptability can mean you adapting to other people to make progress or you being prepared to adapt your origi-nal idea to make it a better one.

The lid's off

Have you had a time in your life when new opportunities seemed to be opening up for you – one opportunity seemed to create a new one, and so it went on? Although you were struggling to keep up with the faster pace of your life, you probably remember it as a fun time.

One opportunity creating another is crucial to the Luck Habit. Fatalists often call this 'serendipity'. Serendipity can also be described as 'a happy accident'. Some people subconsciously refer to it when they say things like 'He was just in the right place at the right time'. Or 'It was fate'. But by saying those things you immediately remove your own personal footprint from the whole process.

Mo Nazam got to play with the pioneering jazz group the Jazz Warriors because he worked very hard to become a great guitar player and they saw that he had something to say musically. The opportunities opened up for him from there because of that hard work.

It's a bit like buying a new car. Suddenly you notice all the other cars like yours on the road. Make a conscious effort to take a particular path in life and you see all the opportunities that the path may offer and, even if you don't, they find you. Mo says:

> 'I started to work with better musicians and through an old friend, bassist Wayne Batchelor, I was able to sit in with the seminal British jazz group of the 1980s, the Jazz Warriors. Founded by Courtney Pine, a lot of the great British players like the Mondesir brothers and Steve Williamson came through that group. A great opportunity had opened up for me. I became a band member although I think they cut me a bit of slack. I wasn't perhaps as technically good at that stage as they were but I think they liked me there because, in my playing, I had something to say. I had a "personality" that gave the sound something different. That balance between technique and individuality is very important in many aspects of life.'

iPrints

If you operate in a commercial environment you will appreciate the importance of new ideas that have value. Here is an example of a great idea. But even better than that, here is an example of a great idea which begat another great idea:

If it's cold and you are wearing gloves you may find it a little difficult to answer your phone, send emails and browse the web, whether you are using a phone or a tablet. One enterprising man, Phil Mundy, based in Leeds, came up with the idea of a small adhesive strip – iPrints – which you can attach to the fingertip of your glove. Marketed initially to the winter sports market, demand quickly spread beyond that (construction workers, people who work in frozen food stores) and the first run of 8,000 strips ran out in two months. A problem begat a great idea, which became a great opportunity and then a growing business.

The crux of this particular story however, is that once you see an opportunity and go live with the idea that supports the opportunity, other opportunities start opening up. Here's what happened next: Phil Mundy recognised a great marketing opportunity at the end of your finger tip and realised that he could produce more revenue from selling ad space there.

You will have experienced something similar in your own life – that sense of a world of new opportunities or experiences opening up to you. Think of a time when a hobby has opened up lots of new opportunities as you explore the possibilities within it. A runner will get better, will be conscious of how much better they are getting, will want to time themself, will join a club, will compete even on a very local level, meet other people who like running, develop a new social life ... the list could go on. The lid is well and truly off.

Playing – summary

- The heart provides the emotional drive to move forward with opportunities but the head provides the necessary counterweight to ill-thought-out, impulsive action. Great decision making comes from 'whole-heart-head-ness'.

- Analyse risk. Risk is fine but have a plan in place to counteract it.

- Be prepared to adapt what you do in a new environment – don't be a rigid thinker, no matter how attached you are to old modes of thinking and practices.

- Opportunities seem to breed. Once you take one, new ones appear out of the old.

- Energy is irreplaceable because passivity means sitting back and waiting for opportunities to arrive. Which they won't. Opportunity spotting and taking is not an armchair sport.

Conclusion

This book presents you with a choice. You can choose to be a player or a spectator.

- **The player** realises that if you want good things to happen to you then you have to do specific things to make those good things happen.
- **The spectator** waits and hopes that the good-luck train will stop by some day. Often you'll hear them loudly complaining when the train takes a different route or is a few minutes early and they just missed it.

Well, the train took a different route because someone else laid a new track. It wasn't early (or late) either. Time is always linked to priority – how you use your time is based entirely on what is most important to you. Those with the Luck Habit always make it a priority to spend their time creating their own luck.

I've been clear that fatalists do two things:

- Use a bad experience as a 'life condition': 'I get all the bad luck and others get all the good luck. Nothing I do makes any difference.'
- Wait for 'good luck' – the lottery win for example – which is a spectacular waste of life.

People with the Luck Habit are hard-nosed realists. They do specific things to give themselves the best chance of success. This book has looked at 20 different Luck Factors to help you do this. From the way you learn to the way you relate to other people. From the way you perform to the way you create purpose in your life. From the way you see opportunity to the way you develop and grow as a person.

You've always had – and always will have – a choice about the way you do these things. Do you want to be an active player in your life or watch it from the sofa? Do you want, at the end of your life, to say 'I had a go' or let all the chances you had to control your own fate slip through your own hands?

It's your choice.

Resources

THE LUCK HABIT IN YOUR ORGANISATION

Douglas Miller Learning has developed one-, two- and three-day Luck Habit seminars for organisations. These can be run for between 10 and 500 people.

Readers who wish to find out more can do so through this email address:

theluckhabit@douglasmillerlearning.com

and/or through the website:

www.douglasmillerlearning.com/theluckhabit

WEBSITES

Jonathan Bond – **www.pinsentmasons.com**

Adam Gee – **www.channel4.com**, **www.arkangel.tv**

Bernice Moran – **www.virgin-atlantic.com**

Mo Nazam – **www.theberakahproject.org**

Michele Rigby – **www.socialfirmsuk.co.uk**

Greg Searle – **www.lane4performance.com/Greg-Searle-Practice-Director.htm**

The story of Greg's comeback at the age of 40 is told in his autobiography, published straight after the 2012 Olympics.

Acknowledgements

There are a few people I would like to thank, since without them I would not have been able to write this book. The first is Elie Williams, my commissioning editor. She championed the initial idea, generated more ideas, fought hard for the book's publication and suggested the title. Thanks Elie. I would also like to thank Laura Blake, who looked after the book once I had submitted the manuscript, and copy editor Josephine Bryan, who got to grips with the manuscript and challenged my inconsistencies and inaccuracies – the remaining errors are my own.

I would like to thank my six interviewees: Jonathan Bond, Adam Gee, Bernice Moran, Mo Nazam, Michele Rigby and Greg Searle. They gave their free time to help me and I am very grateful to them. Where practical, contact details, websites etc. can be found on the previous two pages.

I seem to thank my mentor Mark Brown in every book I write and I would like to do the same here. The mannequin and white light and, I suspect, a few other bits and bobs, were borrowed with my deepest thanks.

Finally, thanks to my local Gosport Library in Hampshire. Libraries create a lovely ambience, not only for reading but for writing too, and that is where much of this book was written.

Index